Digital Information Graphics

Digital Information Graphics

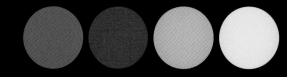

Matt Woolman

With 539 colour illustrations

Thames & Hudson

Contents

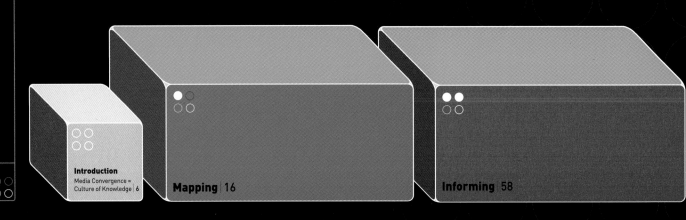

Introduction
Media Convergence =
Culture of Knowledge | 6

Mapping | 16

Informing | 58

Web Cartography | 20

Spherical Spatial Diagrams | 24

Tracking Internet Connectivity | 28

Organic Information Design: Illustrating
Continually Evolving Large Data Sets | 30

Diagrammatic Representations of Data | 38

Three-Dimensional Information Structuring | 40

Mapping Data Paths | 42

Displaying Search-Engine Results | 44

Visualizing Website Structure | 46

MTV2: Connecting the Website
and the Television Channel | 50

Illustrating Web-Session Links | 54

Web Geography | 56

Web Traffic Interpretation | 62

Charting Online Behaviour | 64

Exploratory Data Analysis | 66

Datascapes: The Presentation
and Assessment of Complex Information | 70

Analyzing Search-Engine Findings | 74

Data Classification | 78

Information Landscapes | 82

Immersive Data Display | 84

Linguistic Relationships | 86

Identity Systems | 88

Geographic Comparisons | 90

Monitoring Business Performance | 92

NicheWorks + Exploratory Data Visualizer:
Conveying Information about Large Networks | 96

Interacting | 102

Exploring | 136

Appendices | 172

Web Conversations | 106

Communication Diagrams | 108

Analyzing Semantic Relationships | 110

CS Loom2: Intuitively Visualizing Usenet Newsgroups | 112

Diagramming Group Behaviour | 116

Thought Patterns | 120

CS Visual Explanations: Communicating Critical Issues | 122

Datascapes of Communication | 126

Game Design | 128

Diagramming Software | 130

Graph Manipulation | 132

Digital Nature | 140

User-Controlled Abstract Art | 142

CS Rhizome: An Experimental Online
Environment for New Media Art | 144

Expanding Tree Diagrams | 148

Typographic Play | 150

Visual Experimentation | 156

CS Equator Interdisciplinary Research Collaboration:
Combining the Physical and the Digital Worlds | 160

Dynamic Type | 164

Mapping the Genome | 168

Glossary | 172

Bibliography | 174

Credits and Websites | 174

Index | 176

For Rupert and Calder, who always remind me
that there is an end to the workday.

Acknowledgments:
I would like to thank the following people for their consultation,
generous assistance and contribution to this book. First and
foremost, the researchers, engineers, programmers and designers
who took time out of their busy schedules to correspond with me,
to share their thoughts and ideas and to collect and submit their
work for publication. John DeMao, Anne Graves, Dr Richard Toscan
at Virginia Commonwealth University offered their support and help.

Angeline Robertson gave thoughtful advice, ideas, writing skills
and editorial input. Finally, my thanks to Ursula, my family,
friends and colleagues, who enjoy sifting through the micro
in life for answers to the past and present and maybe for
a glimpse into the future.

This book was funded in part by a generous grant from the Qatar
Foundation, School of the Arts, Virginia Commonwealth University.
Additional support was provided by the Center for Design Studies,
Department of Communication Arts & Design, School of the Arts,
Virginia Commonwealth University.

Introduction
Media Convergence = Culture of Knowledge

Johann Gutenberg's moveable type printing gave thousands access to the power of the written word and spread literacy – and hence knowledge – throughout the Western hemisphere. The printed book, with its bound rectangular pages, typographic syntax (alphabetical symbols arranged linearly into words, sentences, paragraphs) corresponding with grammatical syntax, became the standard format for presenting thoughts and ideas. Not since Gutenberg (1400–68) began working with this technology in the fifteenth century have we been at such a threshold of change in the way information is organized, delivered, received and consumed.

Today's consumer is the progeny of the technology age. No longer simply interested in material goods, he or she now has access to more information than ever and has more input than ever. With increasing awareness and use of information technology, new business practices, higher expectations and the speed at which we demand information and the life cycle of that information, the communication-design industry is undergoing a massive transition from the printing techniques of the past to the innovations and inventions of digital graphic communication. Emphasis is on developing new methods of reaching the right audience with the right content at the right time in the right form and at the right price.

Graphic designers have always operated at the intersection of the material (printed) object and the physical world. However, advancement in digital technologies has transformed this method of print and deliver, which is over 550 years old, into a new model of deliver and print. Communication design no longer

[content] → [design] → [print] → [deliver]
→ [deliver]
→ [deliver]

[content] → [design] → [deliver] → [print]
→ [deliver] → [print]
→ [deliver] → [print]

focuses on the end product – words and images printed on paper – but rather on the system – the processing and display of data. Language and communication have converged with the space and format in which they are presented: email, websites, PDAs, pagers, mobile telephones. Nonetheless, the lifeblood of these methods is still words.

Words make up language. Language is complex and ambiguous. Words are similar to containers that can be filled up with meaning depending on their context. Whether the word 'dog' is spelt 'dog' in English, 'perro' in Spanish, 'chien' in French or 'Hund' in German, it has the same meaning: a domesticated carnivorous animal related to foxes and wolves and raised in a wide variety of breeds. There are other definitions of 'dog': to track persistently, to connect, to avoid, to degenerate, to show off.

Swiss linguist Ferdinand de Saussure (1857–1913) observed that there is only an arbitrary relationship between words (specifically, the thirty-one phonemes that represent the sounds of words in English) and their meaning. In a lecture entitled 'Course in General Linguistics', Saussure declared, 'thought is a shapeless mass, which is only ordered by language'. He bound his ideas into a science known as semiology: the study of systems of signs.

A word is a sign made up of three parts. The syntax, also known as the signifier or form, is the formal or structural relationship between signs, determining the word's appearance. Semantics, also known as

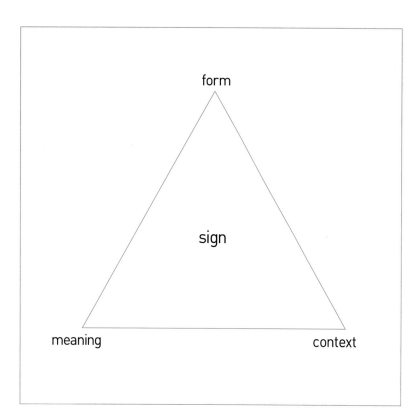

the signified or meaning, explores a sign's relationship with what it represents, defining the word. Pragmatics, also known as function, concerns a sign's relationship to interpreters. It considers the assembly and delivery or content and application of words.

In the relatively short history of graphic design that predates the desktop computer and digital communication, designers were singularly responsible for processing and organizing information into an understandable and deliverable format for a designated audience, a role that placed them in the ambiguous but important realm between thought and language. Technology – photography, typesetting, printing, packaging, distributing – was introduced to the process after the layout had been visualized. Now, digital-communication technologies have uprooted this once centralized role of the designer. The computer processor is a vital component of retrieving, organizing, displaying and transmitting information. Technology is present at all stages of the communication chain, and to a certain extent, the computer processor (and computational algorithms) has replaced the designers' eyes and hands. However, the computer processor cannot be considered as a substitute for designers, rather it should enhance their role.

A new challenge for the graphic designer is to develop the structure of data and the spaces it inhabits into useful visual forms, a challenge akin to the one cartographers faced centuries ago in mapping the earth. Historically, navigators used route maps on land and sea. These consisted of many helpful pieces of information for moving from one place to another, for example, longitude and latitude, elevation, throughways and dead ends. Nevertheless, there is no standard, or ideal, mapping process, a fact that has

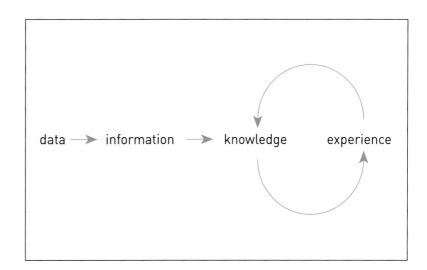

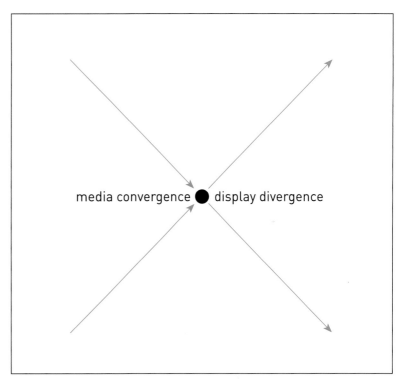

plagued cartographers for hundreds of
years, especially when it comes to mapping the
globe (displaying a three-dimensional object –
a sphere – in two dimensions).

Three approaches map the continents:
Mercator, Gall and Goode. Mercator is the most
widely used and essentially flattens the globe
into a two-dimensional map, a method known
as 'conformal'. The direction and the proximity
between any two points are correct, making it
useful for navigation purposes, but the scale of
objects is distorted. For instance, Mercator is
notorious for equalizing the sizes of Greenland
and South America to conform to its grid
structure. Gall is similar to Mercator
although the exaggeration of land elements
is not as severe. Goode is known as an 'equal
area map' and is laid out on a curvilinear grid,
broken on lines within the oceans, as if one has
taken scissors to the globe and attempted to
cut it to make it flat. While this method maintains
a true scale for land elements, the incisions in
the ocean areas distorts the relationship of
land to water.

The root of information visualization is in graph drawing, which aims to make data easier for human interpretation. If the data elements have a structured relationship, then visualization methods are used to represent them (nodes) and their relationship with each other (edges). If the data elements do not have a structured relationship, then the graphs are used to discover and highlight any relationships. Typical methods of graph drawing include those employed for file and folder hierarchies on desktop computer interfaces, website maps, organizational charts and such project-management charts as PERT (Program Evaluation and Review Technique) and GANTT (developed by Henry L. Gantt).

University research has two approaches to exploring the visual possibilities of information delivery and display. The first is through design schools. For the most part, projects in communication design schools visualize, package and deliver existing bodies of textual and visual information. This approach emphasizes conceptual development, skill building and formal refinement as the student solves a communication problem. However, it also indirectly trains the design student to assume the role of service provider, merely giving form to another's content and information.

Digital tools allow the designer to view individual typographic symbols as actors and typographic composition as cinema. Considerations of typeface, left-to-right linear reading, and top-to-bottom hierarchy have been replaced with anthropomorphic and sculptural characteristics, multidirectional movement and foreground-to-background depth. Eventually, questions arise around the necessity of the designed-for-print, two-dimensional typographic symbols taking on the characteristics of human dancers and actors.

The second approach is through computer-science and engineering schools, which specialize in designing the complex algorithms for gathering, synthesizing and organizing data into often stunning visual form. Yet, in many cases the resulting structures are so complex

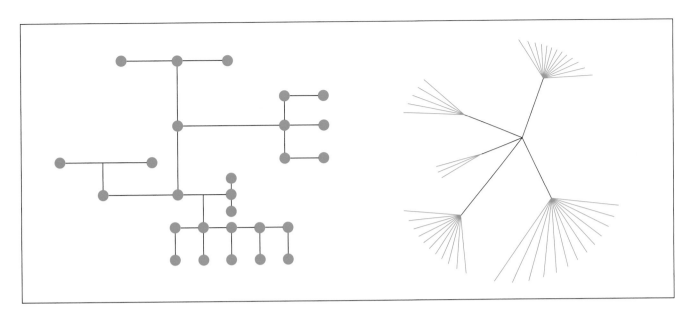

they raise issues of clarity and function. Computer scientists and engineers frequently treat the flat typographic symbol as a label applied to provide some clearness and explanation in a complicated visualization.

The rapid advances in digital technology demand an active dialogue and multilevel collaborations between the design and engineering camps. The way forward is to invent new methods and systems of restructuring data bits into forms that are useful and meaningful to humans and computers. The reasons are simple: functional visualizations are more than innovative statistical analyses and computational algorithms. They must make sense to the user and require a visual language system that uses colour, shape, line, hierarchy and composition to communicate clearly and appropriately, much like the alphabetic and character-based languages used worldwide between humans. Effective visualization is a science and an art, incorporating elements of linguistics, sociology and psychology.

Today's computer technology has the ability to assemble thousands of nodes, and as a result more complex and flexible graphing and layout systems are required by the end-user. Many new methods are displayed on computer monitors, which have their own physical boundaries and limitations. Consider, for example, how any given internet search engine produces results as an endless list of website addresses and other textual information with limited hierarchy. The challenge is to develop ways of arranging the most relevant data in the clearest manner and in the smallest amount of space. The most common of these is the tree structure, which exhibits parent and children data in a similar fashion to the common family-tree layout. The tree can take several forms and many of the examples in *Digital Information Graphics* use some variant of the tree structure, the most important being the classic tree, the H-tree [above, left] and the radial tree [above, right]. Organizing information in a hierarchical manner, with vertical and horizontal readings, the classic tree is much like a family tree:

grandparents sit above parents and parents above children. This format is most commonly used to visualize organizational charts or file–folder hierarchies on computer desktops. The H-tree only differs from the classic tree by allowing multiple reading directions, similar to a road map. Finally, the radial tree positions children nodes radiating in concentric circles around centre (parent) nodes.

The book is divided into four sections – 'Mapping', 'Informing', 'Interacting', and 'Exploring' – and case studies feature within each category. The first section examines the mapping of complex spaces, places, environments and infrastructures, such as the World Wide Web. 'Informing' analyzes the synthesis and visualization of data that can be accessed via the internet and other information stores. The visualization of complex places, events, actions or processes that involve two or more participants, such as an internet chatroom, or gameplay is considered in 'Interacting'. 'Exploring' asks the question 'what if?' and features the studios that are pushing contemporary website interface technology to its limits. The sections are by no means distinct from one another. There are some overlaps, as expected in this vast, dynamic emerging field, and many projects share the same visualization methods. The primary intention of this collection is to identify the principles of data visualization that can be applied to the development of new methods, or in the study of existing methods' effectiveness.

The Principles

Each case study is analyzed in consideration of the following four principles, an understanding of which can be gained from an analogy to architecture. The realization of a building begins with a concept (datum), which comes from the building's intended use. A structure is established that decides the materials and size of the project (wood, brick, single storey, multiple stories). At the same time, the context in which the building is to exist is planned. Systems, spaces and flow channels are developed for humans to navigate and interact with the building.

The principles are arranged to combine systematically the parameters of a problem into new ideas, or, conversely, to break down a solution into constituent parts for analysis. Each principle is a fundamental element for effective information visualization and has one or more parameters defined by a range of characteristics. This is only an initial framework that will most certainly grow and change with the practice of information visualization.

Concept A reference – point, line, plane, volume – to which elements can relate. A fact or proposition used to draw a conclusion or make a decision. This principle has one general parameter:

1.1 referent: abstract or concrete
The ability to link the data set to a physical presence from a human perspective. A concrete referent typically represents a physical space or place, such as a computer network in an office building or a geographic area. Abstract referents include data about social interaction, such as communication between two or more individuals in an internet chatroom, or about semantic information stores, such as a bibliographic database.

 Structure The interrelation or arrangement of parts in an entity; the way in which parts are arranged or put together to form a whole. The data is structured into information. This principle has three parameters:

2.1 relationship: inherent or non-inherent
The methods used to describe the specific relationship among data elements: proximity, height, size, links, demarcation, time and use.

2.2 geometry: flat or spatial
The visual structure of the data for interpretation. 'Flat' indicates a one-dimensional structure, such as a list of websites produced on a search-engine query. 'Spatial' refers to

two- and three-dimensional structures, such as scatter plots (2-D) or virtual-reality environments (3-D).

2.3 scalability: static or dynamic
The ability to update structural information. How adaptable are the parts – can they grow or change over time and/or when new data is incorporated?

Context The space or place in which structure exists, including physical devices for transmission and display. This principle has two parameters:

3.1 representation: literal or metaphorical
The representation of the context in which the structure exists: geographic, cartographic, topological or landscape.

3.2 disposition: detached or immersed
Is the user simply looking at a visualization structure to access information, similar to a road map? Or is the user simultaneously immersed within the structure and experiencing the information?

Navigation The visual and mechanical systems that allow viewers or users to move through information, space or place and to plan, record and control their course and position. This principle has four parameters:

4.1 sign: icon, index or symbol
Visual wayfinding systems and other signifiers, whether typographic elements, graphics, images or shapes.

4.2 perspective: single or multiple
Is the viewer allowed more than one perspective of the structure? Is this controlled by the viewer?

4.3 focus: macro or micro
The ability to increase or decrease the view to provide a general overview or a detailed view of a specific area.

4.4 device: stationary or portable
Is the display device for the structure and
context stationary or is it portable,
thus allowing user mobility?

Information visualization is a rapidly developing
field that includes the use of computer-
generated, interactive, graphic representations
of data to understand complex conditions and
situations, identify relationships and enhance
thought. Most research addresses the subject
from the viewpoint of the computer scientist
or engineer and attempts to be all-inclusive,
if not steeped in technical exclusivity. *Digital
Information Graphics* approaches the field
from the designer's standpoint, assessing the
form, function and application of data with
the aim of communicating information.
The book focuses on the relationship between
data and the visual languages and systems that
convert data into information and knowledge.
The designer has the vital role of data architect,
operating alongside computer scientists and
engineers at the core of the communication
chain and collectively working with the raw
elements of symbols, nodes, edges and
intersections toward the greater goal of
heightening understanding and knowledge
of the digital (and other) worlds in which
we live.

17

Mapping

Mapping

Displaying the projections or routes of large, complex spaces, places, environments and infrastructures, such as the World Wide Web, in simple and comprehensive ways.

A challenge taken up by modern 'digital' cartographers is the mapping of a new kind of world: the World Wide Web. Although there are such physical elements as network lines and routers, computer servers and workstations that serve as the stores and conduits of data (text, static and moving image and sound), there is no distinct reference to the World Wide Web as a large-scale hypermedia system.

The web is based on the concept of distributed client–server architecture. The client is generally an application, such as a browser, that retrieves information stored on computer servers around the world. The information is packaged in the form of a website, which visitors can access, much like a book. However, comparisons to books, magazines, newspapers and other traditional printed and portable formats stop here. A typical visitor's experience of

this complex network is through one or more windows on a computer screen. Travelling from web link to web link is indeed like paging through magazine after newspaper after book, but with no real sense of beginning, middle or end and no physically definable context, such as cover, binding or pages.

Even within a specific website, depending on the sophistication of the site plan and navigation system, users might not fully comprehend where they are, were or will be at any given moment. Humans experience this feeling on a daily basis in other physical forms that are more appropriate comparisons: a shopping mall, an unfamiliar neighbourhood or city, a building under renovation with doorways and pathways re-routed. The situations are endless, but the experiences the same: aimlessness, confusion and frustration.

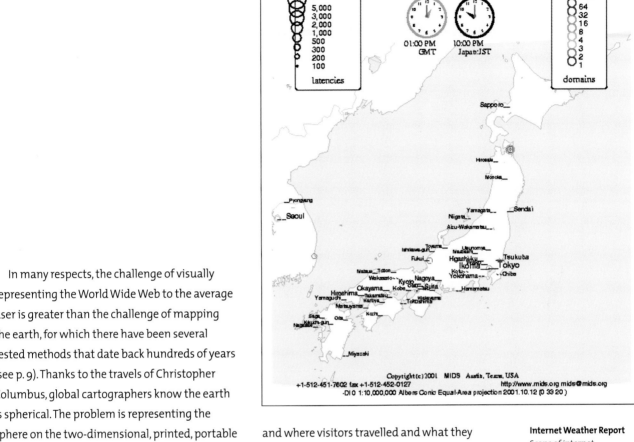

In many respects, the challenge of visually representing the World Wide Web to the average user is greater than the challenge of mapping the earth, for which there have been several tested methods that date back hundreds of years (see p. 9). Thanks to the travels of Christopher Columbus, global cartographers know the earth is spherical. The problem is representing the sphere on the two-dimensional, printed, portable map. There is also a never-ending list of problems that involve boundary and territory shifts as political, religious and environmental events define the course of history, place and space.

It is not possible to say that the World Wide Web is spherical. It can be said that it is dynamic, in constant flux and has a worldwide reach; it is more like a web than a world. Several projects in this chapter engage mapping methods for more site-specific functions – to facilitate website design, development, maintenance and user navigation, and to observe and analyze how a website is used by visitors. On a micro-level, website servers have the ability to collect user data (known as server logs), for example, when

and where visitors travelled and what they requested within a specific site. But, it is simply data. The challenge is to make sense of it, to form it into information and to visualize it in a manner that is useful to humans.

Ranging from commercial to research-based, projects in this chapter assist the website user in comprehending the large, complex and dynamic space we call the World Wide Web. They answer such questions as: where in the web am I? Where have I been? Where am I going? How is my website being used? Are there any parts that are not visited and yet take up valuable space? How can I detect any unwanted infiltration into my website? How can my personal information remain private?

Internet Weather Report
Scans of internet conditions are presented as geographical maps that depict lag or latency, the amount of time it takes to send a packet of data and to receive a response from an internet domain. The report is carried out every four hours.

Website User Paths

VISVIP ('VIS' meaning the 3-D visualization of user navigation paths through a website and 'VIP' standing for Variable Instrumenter Program) was developed by John Cugini and colleagues in the Visualization and Virtual Reality Group (VVRG) at the National Institute of Standards and Technology, US. It is part of the WebMetrics tool set: software designed to assist usability engineers (UE) to evaluate web-based applications by allowing the UE to instruct a website to produce a log of activity on the site. The log is essentially a sequence of time-stamped URLs, indicating the user's path through the website.

VISVIP visualizes paths and automatically lays out a 2-D graph of the website. Each node of the graph represents a webpage, and edges signify links between pages. Nodes are colour-coded: blue for HTML, purple for directories, green for images. Because URLs tend to be long, a short nickname is generated for each page. The UE has several ways to simplify the graph: nodes of a given type, or those not on or near a user path, can be suppressed. Also, if a graph is highly interconnected, the UE can specify that the site be pictured as a tree emanating from a selected root node.

User paths are represented as spline curves, resting on the plane of the website graph. Curvy vertical arrows in and out of the plane mark the beginning and end of each user path. Each user is assigned a unique colour so that several paths can be shown at once. The time spent at each page is depicted as a dotted vertical line with its base at the appropriate node.

The images presented here are sample mappings of a portion of the VVRG website. The user paths are often much more geometrically complex than their structure suggests. Therefore, VISVIP can arrange for the graph to treat pages as adjacent if they are connected by a user path rather than by the existence of a static link. The resulting display makes the structure of the path more straightforward, albeit at the cost of complicating the display of the underlying website.

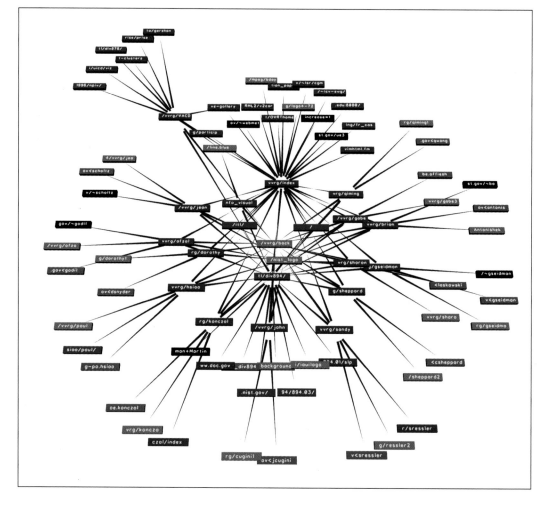

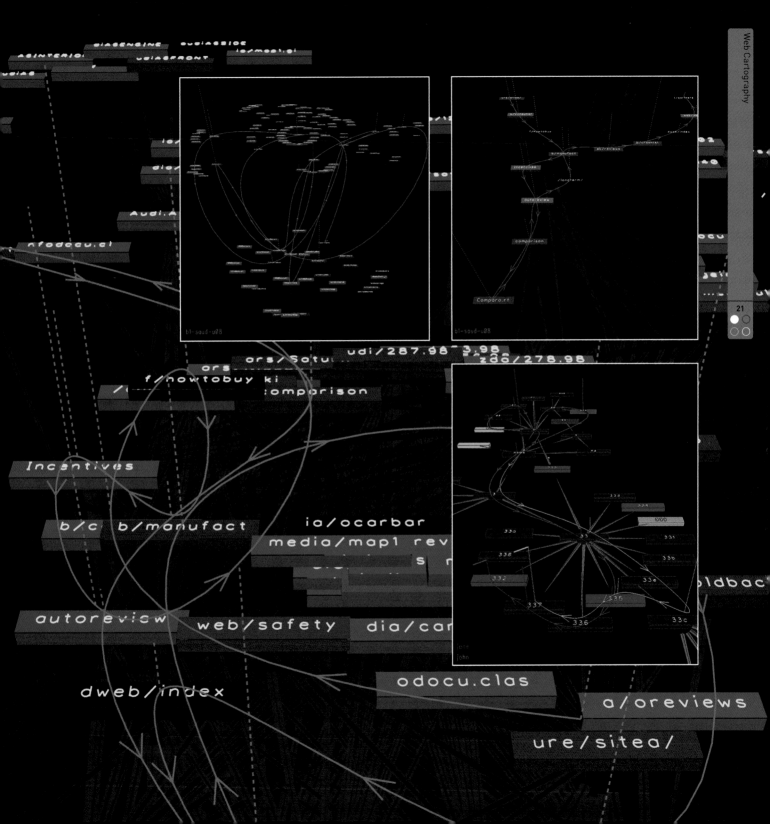

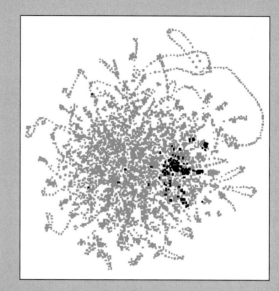

Available segments
365 salonmagazine com salon pagid spacedesc image.ng www2
366 salonmagazine com pagid www2 spacedesc image.ng mothe
367 salonmagazine com media salon circus sept97 pagid image.
368 salonmagazine com pagid spacedesc www2 image.ng salon
369 com altavista query rubberwear web www2 salonmagazine sp
370 research com uk ee information ic www ac lisa ncr us search
371 ncr knowledgelab com lab knowledge index program research
372 parc com research wcs96 xerox go edu page ai bpa papers ari
373 com xerox hearst members parc istl old publications.shtml
374 sims edu berkeley f97 hearst is202 courses outline untitled
375 xerox com pub parcftp qca schuetze edu parc sims genre hea
376 com xerox amazon obidos exec parcftp pub qca 1987-934193
377 kino ch acm schedules programzh sigir home mu page confer
378 ch kino outgreen out dom outinthegreen extras tickets nme s
379 glimpse ch edu cs outinthegreen arizona dom outgreen out s
380 glimpse cs edu arizona hotbot brooksby com london uktravel
381 uk site london londononline co htmlsetupfiles guide the pub
382 uk co islington pubs london webfeet com on travel ucl londor
383 hotbot glimpse pubs com cs results arizona edu page londor
384 olga leo rec pub music songs guitar org indigo_girls ftp inde
385 olga leo pub music songs rec guitar swissair com org rem inc
386 swissair com youthfares vermisst iis_script skysurfer%20fa
387 wimbledon org java score draws 1997 mip scores global.clas
388 pride uk org 97 information 1997 draws ais courses festival d

Find: parc   **Search segments**

Segments matching query "parc":
28 29 30 111 112 121 122 124 234 259 260 261 262 302 303 304 305 309
372 373 375 376 482 504 642 643 644 645 646 649 650 651

Segment 372, Wed 3 Sep 97 11:31:21 to Wed 3 Sep 97 16:50:34
Research
Call for Research Proposals
file:/home/borneo/chalmers/c2.ps
http://ai.bpa.arizona.edu/papers/wcs96/node5.html
References
A Concept Space Approach to Addressing the Vocabulary Problem i
PARC Go Page
PARC Go Page
PARC Go Page
PARC People

Recommendations for segment 372, by neighbours
Hinrich Schuetze [8]
Hinrich Schuetze's Publications [8]
FXPAL People [6]
file://parcftp.xerox.com/pub/qca/otherpub.html [4]
HotBot results: java pipes threads (1+) [4]
AltaVista: Simple Query +Peat +Willett +"limitations of term co-occ
Scientific American: Article: Interfaces for Searching the Web: 03/9
Morgan Price [2]
AltaVista: Simple Query +pedersen +schuetze schutze [2]
Scientific American: Article: Interfaces for Searching the Web: 03/9

Recommendations for segment 372, by cooccurrences
Hinrich Schuetze's Publications [27]
AltaVista: Simple Query +Peat +Willett +"limitations of term co-occ
Hinrich Schuetze [20]
http://www.parc.xerox.com/istl/members/hearst/ [12]
file://parcftp.xerox.com/pub/qca/completepub.ascii [11]
file://parcftp.xerox.com/pub/qca/otherpub.html [11]
file:/usr/java/webdocs/api/java.lang.Long.html#parseLong(java.lang
http://www.bodan.net/meteomedia/progn/zuerich.html [10]
Conclusions and Discussions [10]
Fly-Worm Thesaurus Traversal Experiment [10]

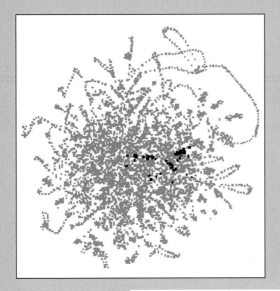

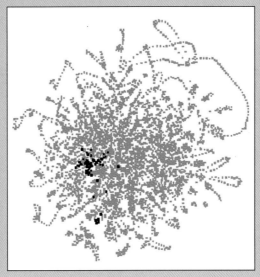

23

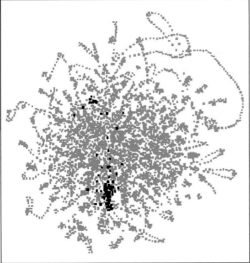

Trailmaps

Matthew Chalmers, professor of computing science at the University of Glasgow, UK, researches the importance of social perceptual issues. He examines the system side – visualization techniques through digital technology – and the theoretical side – relating the complexity of human verbal communication – of computational representation.

Trailmaps aims to access and represent web-based information in a manner that adapts to the activities and interests of individuals within a community of online users. By continually logging the names or identifiers of the information objects through which users move, a path is constructed showing past activity. The path concentrates on usage history as opposed to content analysis. By placing activity at the centre of the representation and not on the periphery, the path focuses on the reader rather than the author

and the browser rather than the site.

First, a recommender system called 'Recer' (pronounced with a hard 'c') is employed, which analyzes a user's ongoing activity on the internet and creates a sliding window that logs the changes to a web browser's history. Entry to every site adds a timestamp and URL to a chronologically ordered file: the path file. If a user selects a URL or title, the segment browser sends a request to the web browser to access the associated URL, thus feeding back into the ongoing logging and recommendation process. The recommender reminds users where they have been before, recommending useful symbols, such as web URLs, program file names and words, based on user paths.

A 'stop list' filters out homepages of search engines, advertising sites and even GIF files, which are used more frequently as buttons and icons. Each window shows a segment of the path and the set of URLs

it contains. The last and most recent path segment is then compared against all earlier segments to find a ranked list of recommendations (things to read, places to go). The neighbour method offers more specific recommendations because it produces its results only from the areas that closely match the target segment and not from the entire data set's statistics.

The recommender system is like an automatic breadcrumb dispenser that reminds travellers where they have been before. The user may edit out any points along the path that are not useful or might be sensitive to other users. Since these paths are associated with people and their decisions (as opposed to content), they present the community's use of, and association with, information.

The images shown here map ten weeks of web surfing by Matthew Chalmers and his colleagues.

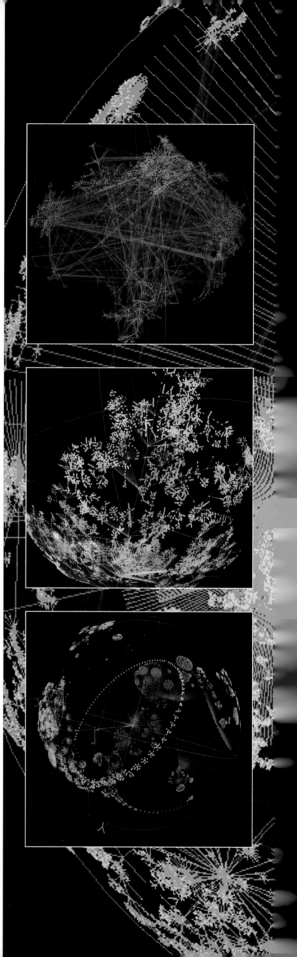

Walrus

Developed by CAIDA, US, Walrus visualizes large graphs in three-dimensional space. Walrus is able to display graphs containing a million nodes or more, but visual occlusion, due to clustering and overlapping in a small space, can diminish its visual effectiveness. Therefore, the tool is best applied to medium-sized graphs that are clearly defined trees, for example, a graph with a hundred-thousand nodes and a slightly larger number of links. The layout is based on a user-supplied spanning tree – a graph that is inherently hierarchical as opposed to one that establishes an arbitrary order.

Hyperbolic geometry is used to depict the graphs inside a sphere. Objects near the sphere's centre are magnified, while those near the boundary are shrunk, as if in a fisheye-lens distortion. The level of magnification and visible detail varies across the display due to its spherical nature, allowing the user to examine the fine details of a small area while always having a view of the whole graph as a frame of reference.

The images on these pages feature graphs of different sizes and complexity: some are network topology graphs, ranging in size from 10,000 to 500,000 nodes; others represent CAIDA's website directory hierarchy (about 14,000 nodes) and directory trees.

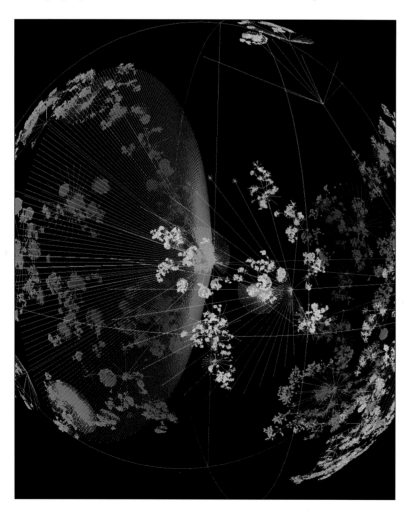

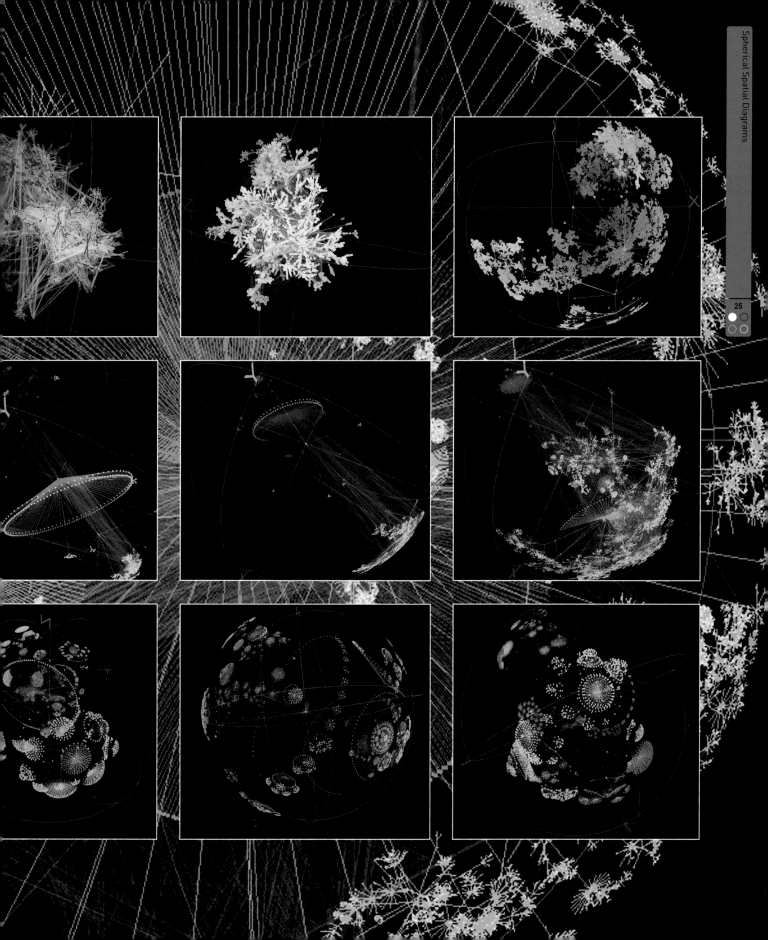

1
Hyperbolic Space

Tamara Munzner, a graduate student in the Computer Graphics Laboratory at Stanford University, US, investigates the use of hyperbolic space in visualizing information on the internet. A system of nodes and links are projected into a hollow, transparent sphere, known as the 'sphere of infinity', providing a means of browsing the page-link structure of a typical website.

Visitors manipulate the elements and rotate the chart inside the sphere to view different perspectives. A unique aspect of the hyperbolic structure means that specific details and the overall context is visible at any given time, a state achieved by giving preference to objects in the centre of its spherical space. Consequently, as objects are moved into the periphery, they shrink in size and at the edge of the sphere the nodes are very small.

1 This shows part of the Stanford graphics group website laid out as a graph in 3-D hyperbolic space. The entire site has over 20,000 nodes, 4,000 of which are drawn from the papers archive. The tree is oriented so that a node's ancestors appear on the left and descendants on the right.

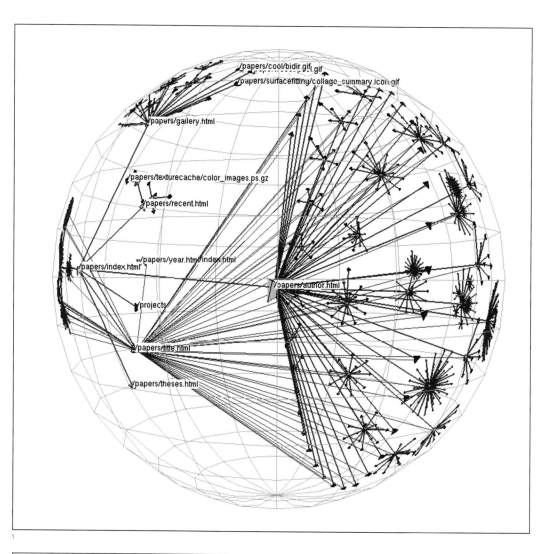

1

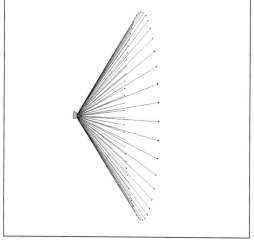

2a

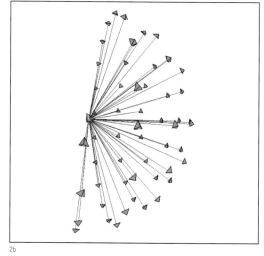

2b

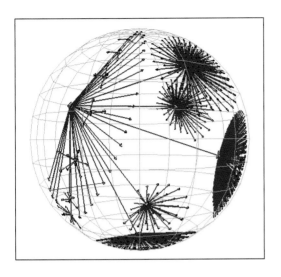
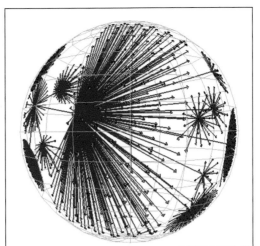

Hyperbolic Space

2 Munzer compares the traditional cone-tree layout along the circumference of a circle [**2a**] with the hyperbolic-space layout on the surface of the sphere [**2b**]. The traditional layout requires a large cone radius and is very sparse; the hyperbolic-space structure only needs a small cone radius and the layout is denser.

3 Hyperbolic motion through the generations of a 2,000-node Unix file system is illustrated in this sequence. The structure contains over two hundred files.

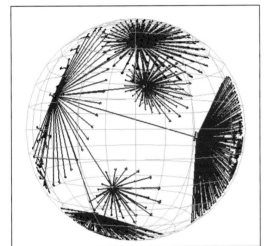
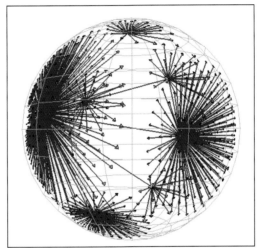

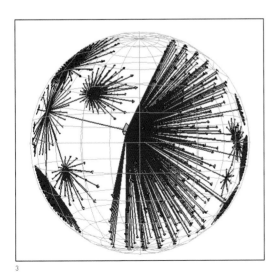
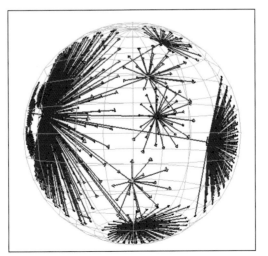

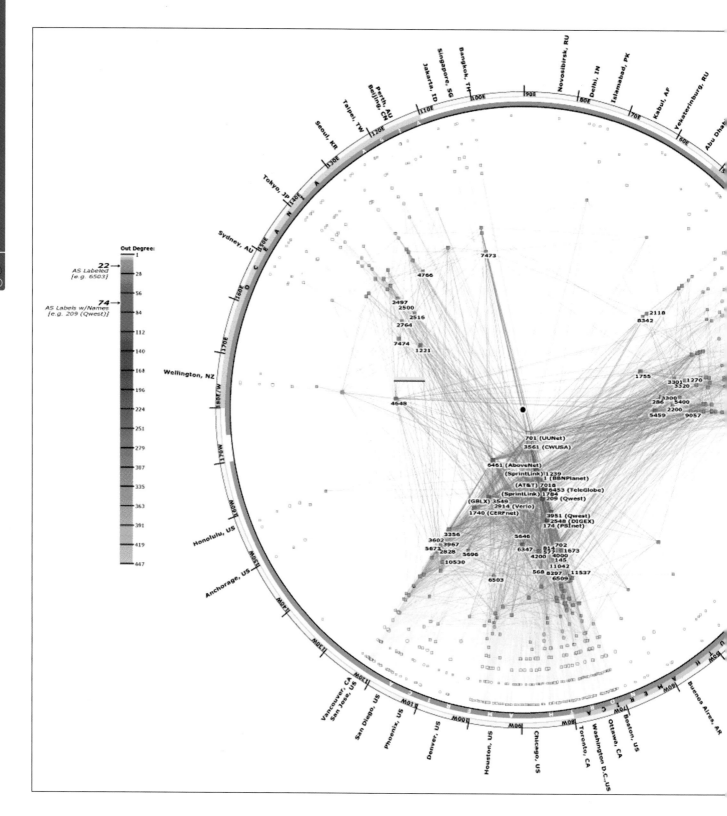

Out Degree:

22
AS Labeled
[e.g. 6503]

74
AS Labels w/Names
[e.g. 209 (Qwest)]

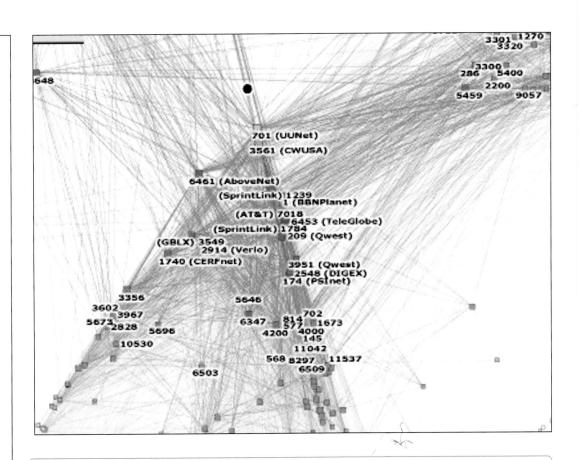

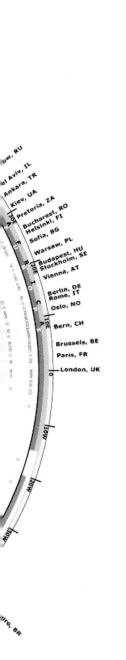

Cooperative Association for Internet Data Analysis (CAIDA)

Observing internet traffic was fairly easy when the net was first set up. During the 1990s, however, the web grew at an incredible rate and tracking connectivity became almost impossible. CAIDA (a programme at the University of California's San Diego Supercomputer Center, US) researchers have produced a detailed visualization of the relationships between and locations of autonomous systems (ASES), which are vital components of internet infrastructure and route connectivity through the

internet in much the same way as roadway intersections route vehicles. The aim of the map is to find out how highly complicated internet connectivity is distributed among internet service providers (ISPS).

Presented here are macroscopic snapshots of the internet core taken from data collected during a two-week period in mid-January 2000. One of CAIDA's goals is to develop techniques that illustrate relationships and depict critical components within the internet infrastructure.

The graph shows 626,773 IP (internet protocol) addresses and 1,007,723 IP links (immediately adjacent addresses in a traceroute-like path) of data from sixteen monitors examining approximately 400,000 destinations over 52% of globally routable network prefixes. CAIDA mapped each IP address to the AS responsible for routing it.

Graphing website relationships and geographic information shows the concentric nature of ASES based in North America. ISPS in Europe and Asia have

many relationships with ISPS in the US, but there are not many direct links between ISPS in Asia and Europe. Technical (cabling and route placement and management) and policy (business models, geo-political considerations) factors all contribute to the final graph.

The overall form is visually stunning, with a complex array of colour-coded threads and connections. The structure is static and the visitor views the map externally.

Organic Information Design
Illustrating Continually Evolving Large Data Sets

The methods used to design static chunks of data – charting, graphing, sorting – are well understood, but innovations are yet to be developed for examining dynamic sources of data or very large data sets. Ben Fry, a researcher in the Aesthetics and Computation Group at the MIT Media Lab (US) with a background in computer science and graphic design, is building systems that create interesting visual constructions from large bodies of information. His system designs treat individual pieces of data as living and growing elements in an environment. Known as organic information design, this concept is addressed in Fry's software experiments Valence, Tendril and Anemone.

Project Title: Valence

Concept According to Fry, the premise of his research is that the best way to understand a large body of abstract information, whether it be a 200,000-word book, data from a website, or information on a financial transaction between two multinational corporations, is to offer a feel for general trends and anomalies in the data by presenting a qualitative slice showing how the information is structured and changes over time. The most important information comes from supplying a context and setting up the interrelationships between the data elements. In Valence, Fry applied this method to visualize user traffic on a website (p. 33) and word use and frequency within a passage from *The Innocents Abroad* by Mark Twain (pp. 31–32).

Structure In the Twain example, Fry extracts words from a traditionally formatted block of text, which appears as a ghostly apparition in the background. The frequency with which a word appears dictates its position on the diagram: most-used words make their way to the outside of the structure, pushing less-common words to the centre.

The words in the website example were replaced by webpage URLs so that instead of a typical web report comprised of bar charts and including such obvious information as '20,000 people visited the homepage', the software actually builds a continually evolving map of how people have been using the site. The data in both examples has a non-inherent relationship, which allows greater flexibility in visual structure.

The map's layout depends on traffic patterns rather than the structure put in place by the site's designer, thus providing additional information on how well the site has been built. Words are connected by razor-thin links that follow spherical orbits in a 3-D structure.

Context The examples of Valence take the form of plantlike organisms suspended in dark 3-D space. The background text in the Twain project is a curtain from which the structure emerges, reinforcing spatial dimension and depth.

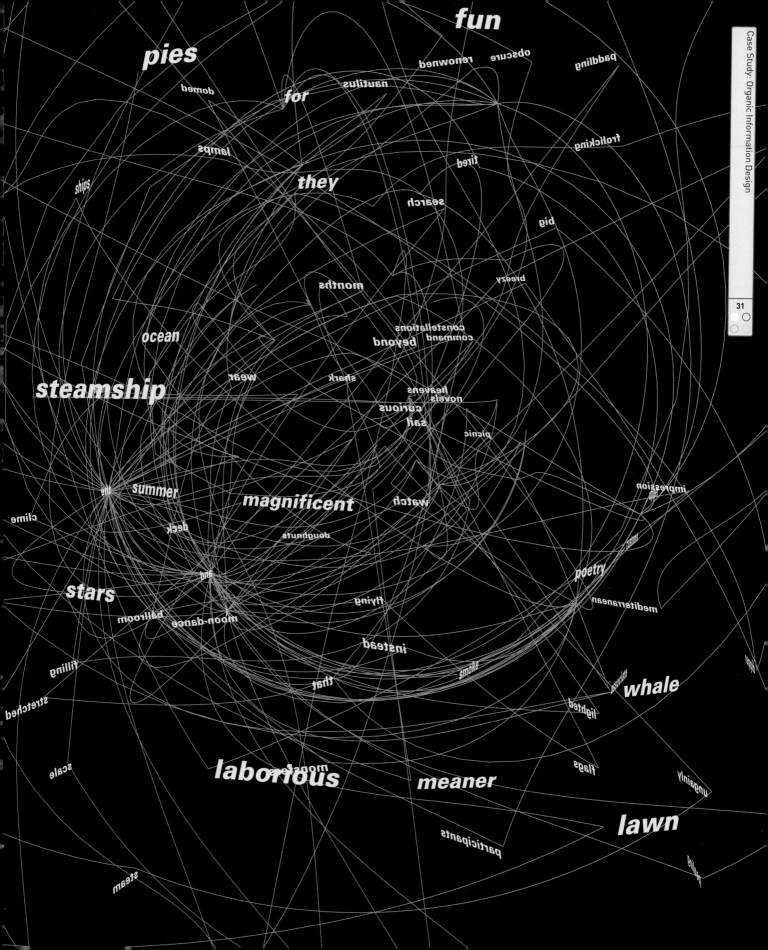

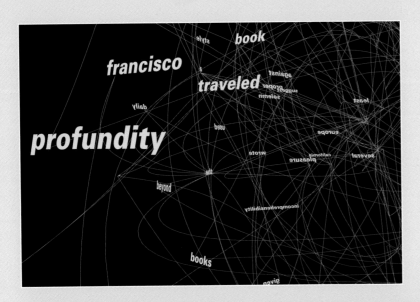

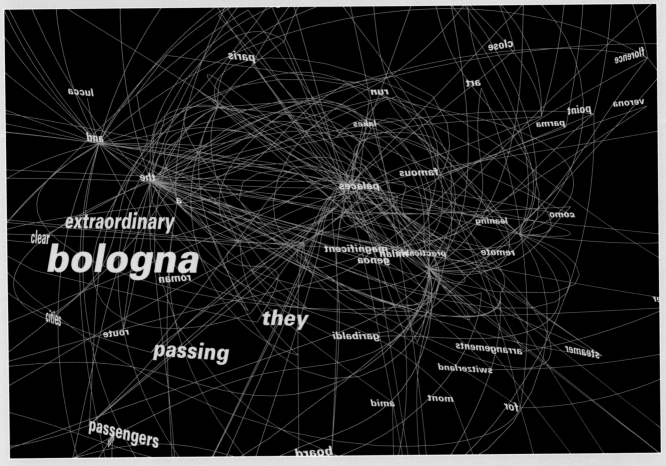

Navigation The main structure's clarity and volume allows the viewer to visually swim through Valence, identifying specific links and pathways between words and website URLs. Various vantage points and focus views give more detail and simulate volume and depth within the structure.

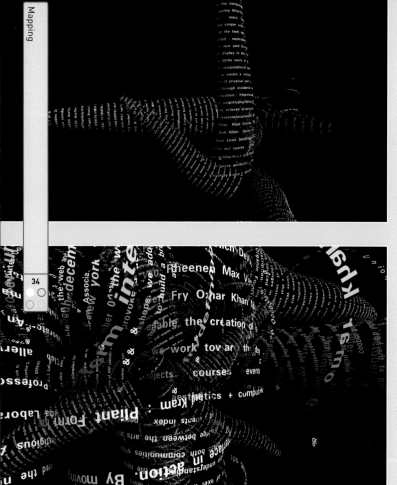

34

Project Title: Tendril

Concept Tendril is an experiment in building a dynamic typographic structure out of abstract, but text-based, information. Operating in a similar manner to web crawlers or robots, Tendril first reads a webpage, then assembles a list of all the page links.

Structure The information that Tendril uses is related by links built into the website. It generates a branch – or tendril-like structure – from the text content of a webpage. Words and phrases spiral to enclose volumes of

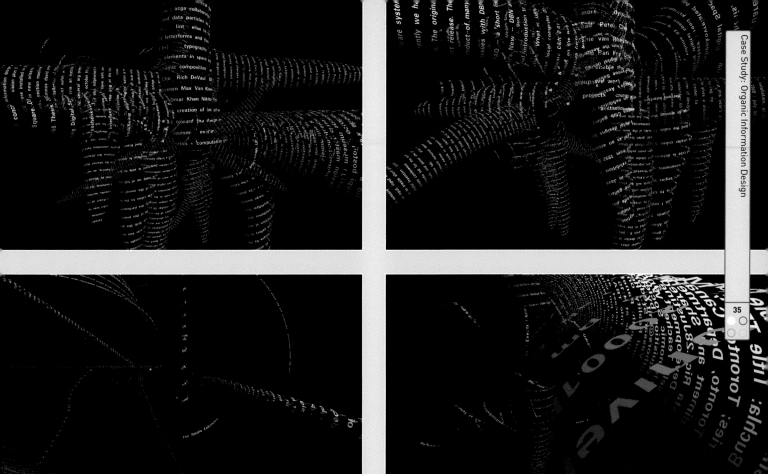

space and to form branches of various thickness. This process is repeated for each of the linked pages, with the branches attaching themselves to the main system. An enormous branching arrangement grows over a period of time, its molecular structure formed from the letters, words and phrases that are contained in the set of connected webpages. Tendril was created using the programming languages Java, c++ and openGL.

Context Emphasizing its complexity and structure, Tendril is suspended in a dark space. The viewer is outside the structure looking in, but increases in

scale give the viewer a sense of flying inside the display.

Navigation Letters, words and phrases are the only means of navigating the information. The spaces between the letters and words, combined with focus, transparency and colour, provide a sense of 3-D volume. The viewer's eyes easily navigate the complexity of these structures from a single vantage point.

Project Title: Anemone

Concept Illustrating how individuals travel through a website, Anemone gives a molecular view of what is happening on a site by assembling a body of abstract data. It goes on to highlight patterns and relationships across time and across the structure of the webpages.

Structure Anemone reveals only those parts of a site that receive visitors. It reads a website usage log and sequentially maps the activity as a 2-D visualization. A visited page is a simple white tentacle node on the map, connected by branches that show the underlying hyperlink structure.

The first rule of 'digital nature' Fry built into his system is that tentacles increase in girth as more visitors hit a specific page, making them more visible on the map. To balance this rule, he has incorporated an 'atrophying' aspect – when webpages stop receiving visitors their nodes gradually wither away and eventually

disappear from the map. Branches of Anemone are placed close to each other, but without any visual overlapping. These dynamic rules result in a map that quivers and flutters.

Context Fry chose a branching, growing organism to illustrate the integration of page structure and dynamic usage data. The white tentacles of the individual webpages are linked by faint, orange pathways that form the three-dimensionality of the structure.

Navigation As with Valence and Tendril, the viewer is positioned outside the structure. Text labels assist the viewer in identifying the websites and associated links, but the primary signifiers are the white tentacle nodes and orange pathways. Multiple perspectives can be seen from the same vantage point, and greater detail emerges when the structure is enlarged.

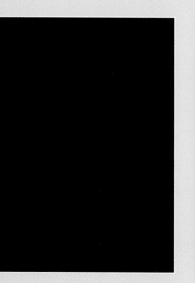
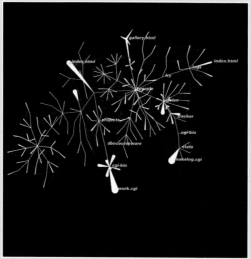
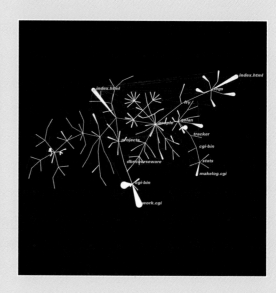

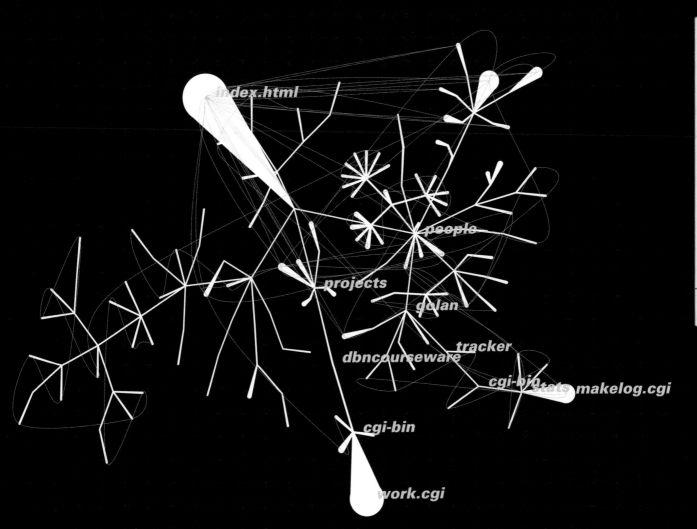

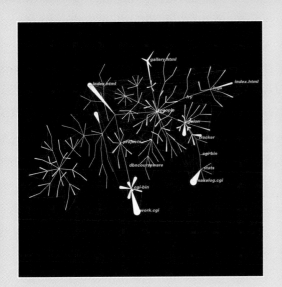

*the*TableLens*experience*→ hot

Table Lens is a revolutionary technology that allows end users to interact with data directly.

Ameritrade & Table Lens
makes it easy to analyze Mutual Funds

RECENT HOT TOPICS

2000 USA Census
See how the census affected the allocation of seats in Congress.

California Crisis
Refrigerators use 1/6th of household energy. Compare the energy usage data for different models.

StarTree
The fastest way to

Ameritrade has chosen to use Table Lens as a premium service for their Mutua

Jim Ditmore, Ameritrade's CIO, is excited about adding Inxight's Table Lens Server to the new Supermarket product. "This will enable Ameritrade clients to quickly and accurately review and fund information and make educated investment decisions."

| Click here | to highlight an amazing money making fund!

Try sorting by clicking on ea header:
1) "Quarter to Date"
2) "Year to Date"
3) "5 years"

	1- Lipper Fu...	4- Fund C...	6-Index n...	1 Month	Quarter t...	Year to Date	1 Year
1	LBDT	XI	Lipper Mg...	15.7	13.06	81.86	81.86

Disclaimer

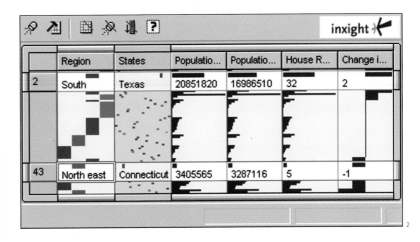

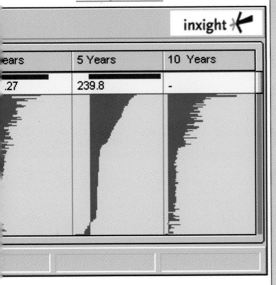

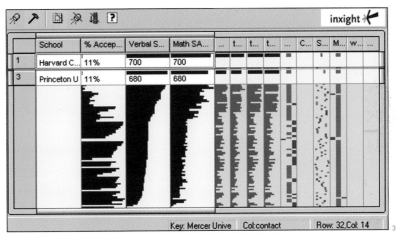

1–3
TableLens™

Located in Santa Clara, California, US, Inxight Software, Inc. develops information-access and content-visualization software for automating the analysis, organization and presentation of information across intranets, extranets and the internet. Based on more than twenty years of research at the Xerox Palo Alto Research Center, Inxight's products are designed for information-intensive applications in enterprise markets,

including financial services and electronic publishing. Users can identify, extract and analyze relevant information from large amounts of networked and complex data sites. The software uses highly visual navigation methods.

Inxight TableLens generates graphical displays of tabular data, even information that is too large to view and understand in traditional table formats. Capable of presenting over 100 columns and 65,000

rows of data on a single computer screen, the software forms interactive data visualizations, permitting users to identify patterns and trends that would otherwise require extensive, time-consuming data analysis. Presented here is information about the performance of over one thousand mutual funds [1], how the US 2000 census affected the allocation of seats in Congress [2] and US college acceptance criteria [3].

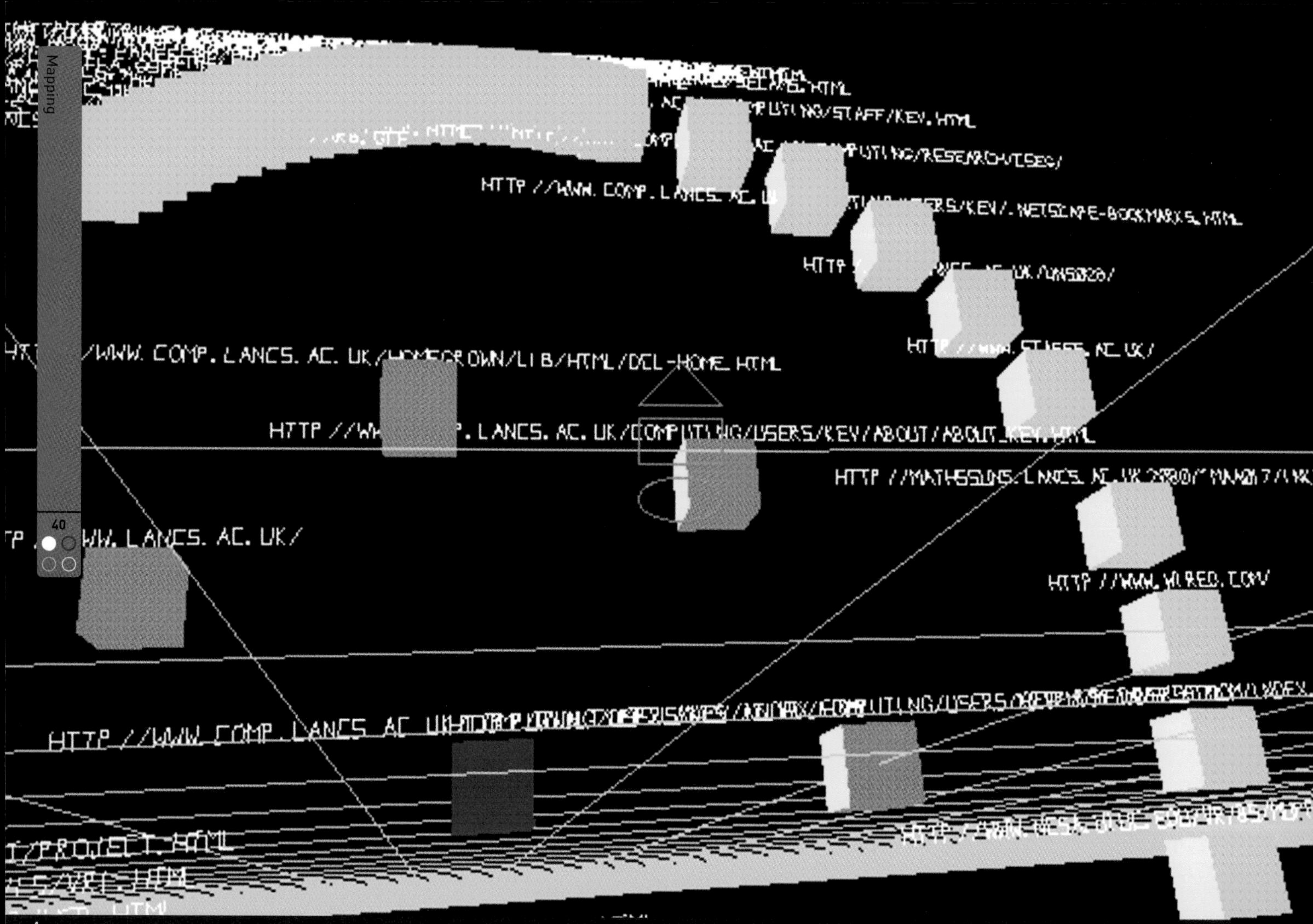

40

HANDLE-SELF.HTML

...AC...PUTING/STAFF/KEV.HTML

...PUTING/RESEARCH/SE5/

HTTP //WWW. COMP. LANCS. AC. U...

...TING/USERS/KEV/.NETSCAPE-BOOKMARKS.HTML

HTTP ...FF. AC.UK./UNS028/

...XB. GTF. HTML ...NTIE...

HTTP //WWW. COMP. LANCS. AC. UK/HOMEGROWN/LIB/HTML/DCL-HOME.HTML

HTTP //WWW.STAFF.AC.UK/

HTTP //WW...P. LANCS. AC. UK/COMPUTING/USERS/KEV/ABOUT/ABOUT_KEV.HTML

HTTP //MATHSSUNS/LANCS. AC. UK 2780/MANON 7/1 W...

TP ...WW. LANCS. AC. UK/

HTTP //WWW.WIRED.COM

HTTP //WWW. COMP. LANCS. AC. UK/HOME...COMPUTING/USERS/KEV...

HTTP //WWW. COMP. LANCS. AC. UK...

...T/PROJECT.HTML

...CT.HTM

1

1–5
URLGRAPH

Kevin Palfreyman (UK) focuses on providing simple, presence-awareness protocol for such large distributed information systems as the World Wide Web. URLGRAPH is Palfreyman's abstract visualization of information stores, depicting a limited cross section of the World Wide Web in a 3-D geographical manner to facilitate collaborative browsing of the data.

In URLGRAPH, Palfreyman builds web navigation aids by using novel layout techniques in the 3-D space of virtual reality (VR). This involved extending the abilities of VR software tools to allow the visual elements, represented as simple 3-D shapes in the 3-D environment, to possess and to be capable of fetching URLs. He went on to implement a number of 3-D layout algorithms and then investigated which attributes best aided the navigation of web space. The initial visualization uses a spanning tree algorithm, laid out in concentric circles, and adapted to handle graphs rather than just trees.

A partial tree layout is shown here [2]. Nodes are represented as black dots, links are black lines and the root node is in the bottom right corner and points to four more nodes that are equally spaced around it. Each of the four nodes at the apex of the bright-red area points to a further four nodes, which are shown at the top of the bright-green areas. In the diagram, the short cyan lines indicate the size of the gap that is left between the subgraphs (the sets of links and nodes that connect to a single node, the 'parent' or 'root' node) of sibling nodes. The light-coloured sections indicate open space for additional nodes in the future.

The first graphical implementation of URLGRAPH is V1.2 [1, 3–5], which maps movement around the web from Palfreyman's homepage. Links are visualized in the 3-D environment. The walk depth used is the default, meaning that the root URL is visited and then each of the URLs referenced from that page are also visited. The root node is shown in red, the level one nodes in orange and the level two nodes in yellow. The links appear in the same colour as the node from which they stem. The viewer can move through the structure and read the data, with the 3-D characteristics indicating the size of the data and the speed of data acquisition.

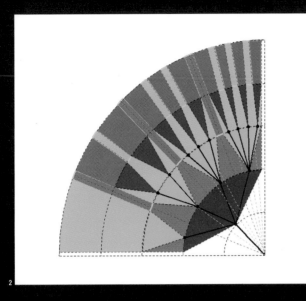

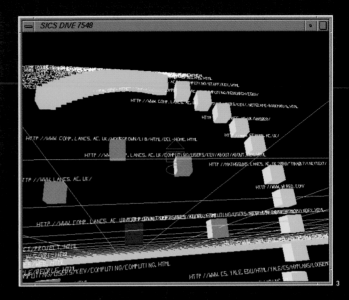

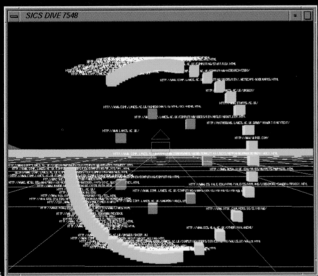

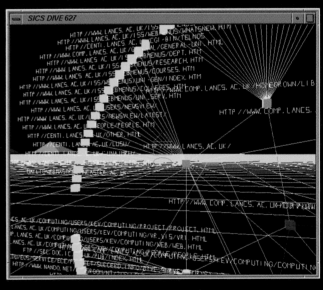

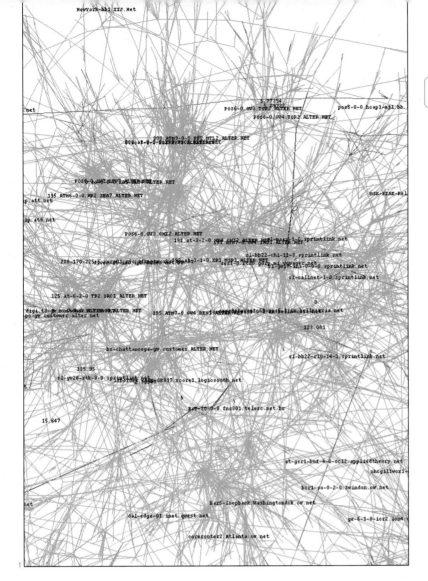

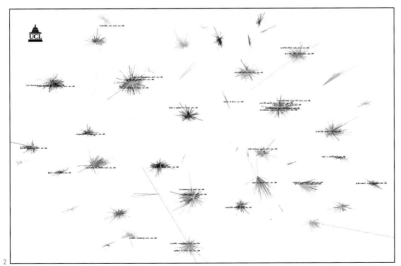

1–3
Traceroute Software

Stephen Coast (UK) has developed an application known as a 'traceroute'. As Coast describes on his website, 'When you send or receive data over the internet your computer does not care which pathway (wire, optic fibre) or route (Hong Kong, Urbana-Champaign) the data travels. These are irrelevant as long as waiting time is not an issue.' Of course, we do mind waiting, so routers have been designed to move data packets over the fastest link and the shortest distance possible.

The travel routes of internet data are all but invisible to the human user and it is in this respect that traceroute software is valuable. The application sends out packets of data that are programmed to self-destruct after the data has visited a certain number of computers. Each time a packet visits a website server it dies and the computer returns a message that the packet is no longer in existence. The computers that report these deaths identify themselves to the traceroute software, which records the information in a database file. The specific data gathered and recorded is the route between the original computer and the destination computer, the network identity of each computer and the time it took the data to travel that

route. POVRAY software renders the gathered information into 3-D form, while Mathematica software runs statistical functions and generates 2-D graph structures.

Data structures are composed of lines (data-packet pathways) and spheres (the destinations of the data packets); the line length and sphere size indicate the speed at which the data packet is travelling and the number of edges (the relationships between nodes), respectively. They are complex objects that can be animated for the viewer to fly around and through. The viewer can control his or her flying direction and distance to or from the data structure.

1 A mapping of the entire internet, with 32,000 recorded nodes. The dense areas (top left) are US nodes and UK nodes are shown in the lower middle of the map.

2 Each cluster represents a department at University College London, with lines showing inter-departmental links.

3 These visually intriguing diagrams show data sent from Stephen Coast to random IP addresses (website servers). Each node visited, along with all the links extending from that node, is recorded by the traceroute software.

Self-Organizing Maps

The WEBSOM research group is led by Emeritus Professor Teuvo Kohonen of the Academy of Finland at the University of Technology (HUT), Helsinki. Kohonen and his team investigate such areas as the theory of self-organization, associative memories, neural networks and pattern recognition. WEBSOM automatically organizes miscellaneous collections of text documents into meaningful maps for exploration. It is based on the SOM (Self-Organizing Map) algorithm that visualizes and interprets large, high-dimensional data sets, arranging the documents on a 2-D grid with related documents appearing close to each other. SOMs are typically used to visualize such things as financial results because they can represent the central dependencies within the data on the map.

Presented here are visualizations of a web search engine. The top level shows general topics, the next level down lists subtopics, and so on. The map consists of a regular grid of 'neurons' or processing units. A model of some multidimensional observation is associated with each unit. The map attempts to depict all the available observations with optimal accuracy, placing alike models close to each other and dissimilar ones far apart.

To view the contents of the documents, the user must click on the map's white points or 'pigeon-holes'. Complete texts can be searched to find an interesting starting point for browsing. Clicking on a particular part of the map, zooms in on that area, while arrows direct users to adjacent units where similar texts are located. Texts are read by clicking on the headings. The labels on the map are an example of the core vocabulary within that area. Shading indicates the density of documents within a particular area, with light zones containing more documents. For the purpose of simplicity, website addresses and general topic headings are abbreviated.

WEBSOM zoomed map - Million documents

Click arrows
to move to neighboring areas on the map, and to move up to the overall view.

Explanation of the symbols on the map

bionet - bionet.announce
blues - rec.music.bluenote
books - rec.arts.books
classical - rec.music.classical
humor - rec.humor
movies - rec.arts.movies.past-films
neurosci - bionet.neuroscience
philosophy - comp.ai.philosophy
philosophy.tech - sci.philosophy.tech
plant - bionet.biology.plant
proge - rec.music.progressive
robotics - comp.robotics

Click any white dot to enter the node.

Instructions

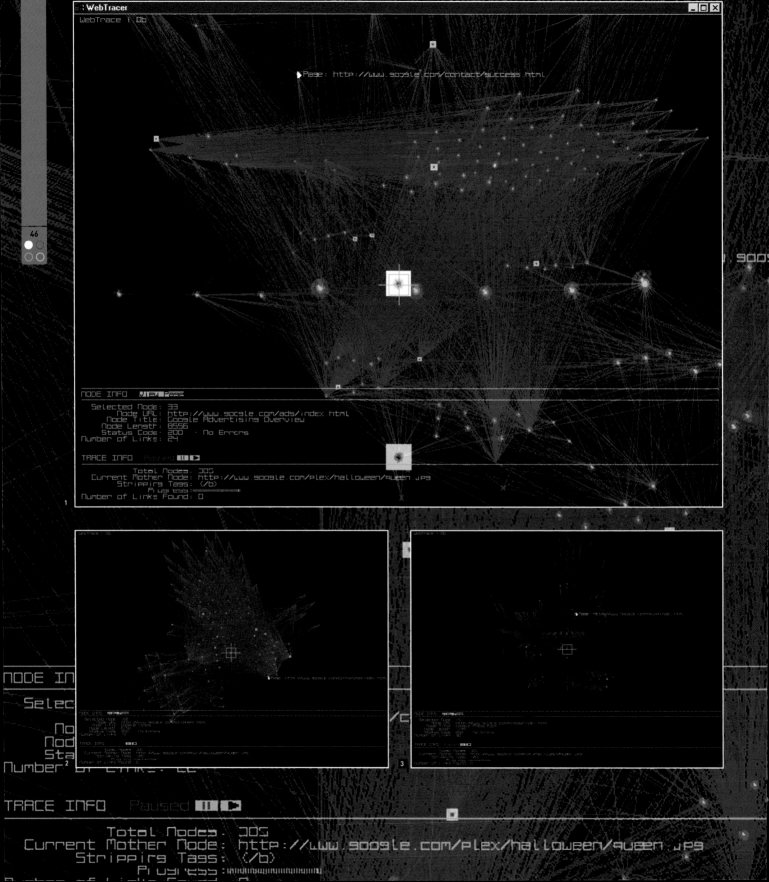

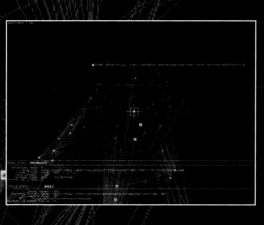

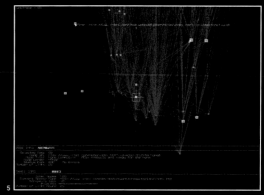

1–6
Webtracer

Countless applications assess websites for structural integrity and educational purposes, but few illustrate the visual structure that web hypertext creates. Webtracer, released by NullPointer (UK), represents this structure as a 3-D molecular diagram that can be examined from any angle and any distance. Pages are nodes (atoms) and links are the strings (atomic forces) that connect the nodes to each other. The images here are visualizations of the website structure for the search engine Google (400 nodes, **1–3**) and the company site for Intel (400 nodes, **4–6**).

Nodes can be selected to gain further information on their content and a browser is launched to visit the corresponding page directly. The molecular structure of the site reflects the sequence of hyperlinks within actual pages and the internal structure of the host site's file system.

Webtracer generates an interactive molecular vector-based diagram →

that is unique to each site it visits. Information-design tendencies and the intentions of the site designer to promote or demote certain types of information are made visually obvious. The resulting forms range from deeply interwoven tapestries to delicate and simple tree designs. It is intended as an interactive tool to visualize the web and allow users to gather information about a site through its structure and design. Shown here are visualizations of the website structure for Rhizome (**7–9**, see p. 144) and Microsoft [**10–12**].

Page: http://www.nullpointer.co.uk/+/ty0

7

8

WebTrace 1.0b

Page: http://www.microsoft.com/info/copyright.htm

NODE INFO **VIEW PAGE**

Selected Node: 60
Node URL: http://www.microsoft.com/worldwide/
Node Title: No Title
Node Length: 0
Status Code: 0   · No Errors
Number of Links: 0

TRACE INFO   Paused ■■ ■▷

Total Nodes: '100
Current Mother Node: http://www.microsoft.com/catalog/display.asp?subid=220&site=10587
Stripping Tags: <TD>
Visual tss :||||||||||||||||||||||||||||||||||||||||||||||||||||||||
Number of Links Found: 7

10

/fresh
Ls--An

Status Code: 200   · No Errors
er of Links: 33

E INFO   Paused ■■ ■▷

Total Nodes: '100
rrent Mother Node: http://rhizome.org

WebTrace 1.0b

11

rview with Germaine Koh

ct.rhiz?2224

MTV2
Connecting the Website and the Television Channel

Established in 1996, Digit is an interactive design consultancy based in London that specializes in innovative interfaces and games for internet and CD-ROM. MTV Europe charged Digit with the challenge of creating a website – MTV2 – that would connect a wider audience to the television channel by using an expansive database listing alternative music videos. Visitors to the website can assemble their own video playlist to be featured on the MTV2 channel. The work Digit produced for MTV2 was also adopted for the television station's on-air graphics system.

Concept The MTV2 UK website is intended to map out the site's purpose and to provide interaction with MTV2's television programming. Correlating the theme of the channel – music and videos – with that of the website was very important, and MTV wanted to encourage more people to return to the television channel. Digit put forward a twofold proposal: to create a sense of community and also to find a 'real' space that MTV2 could occupy.

Structure The site is divided into four components: 'Info', 'Playlist/Schedule', 'Create' and 'Community'. In 'Create' the user becomes VJ, accessing MTV2's complete database to programme an hour to be shown on the channel. 'Community' enables users to read or write commentary from or about other users and MTV2 itself. 'Playlist/Schedule' features the programme schedule and the MTV2 Recommends Chart with current video reviews and a chart of the most-played videos. 'Info' allows the viewer to contact MTV2 and explains the site's different components. The website is more about mapping the site's purpose and linking it to the television station than it is about flat pages of information to click on. It establishes a sense of community among its many devoted fans, one of whom visits the video-programming feature every twenty seconds.

Context Inspiration for the site's graphic style came from an axonometric construction diagram for a desk. The resulting interface is a set of interlocking blocks that are colour-coded to correspond to different areas of the site and to permit easy navigation. The four components are represented volumetrically to show relative importance. The website was designed using Flash 4 and is accessible on the internet. Each area uses a Flash illustration to keep the feeling of solidarity and density.

Navigation A simple click of the mouse moves the viewer through the space. Away from the homepage, a horizontal menu at the bottom left of the screen is comprised of four coloured cubes, corresponding to the site's different areas, that direct the user to any part of the site. The website design combined with the on-air graphics has resulted in a seamless integration of MTV2 online and MTV television.

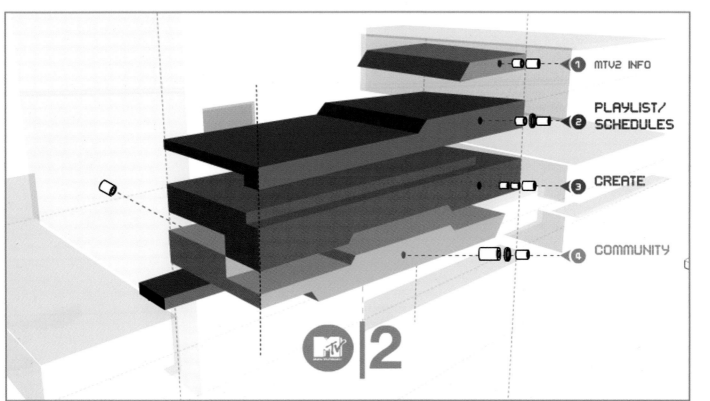

1

  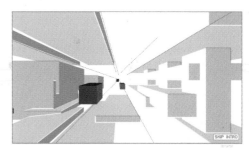

2

1

Clearly laid out, the 3-D image on the homepage maps the site's structure.

2

The website's introduction sequence.

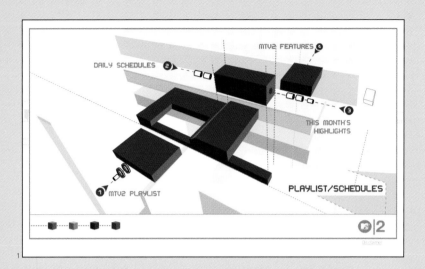

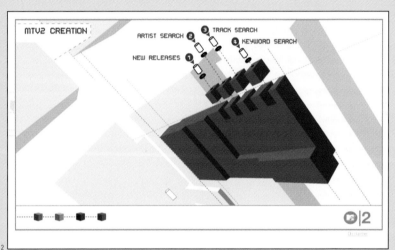

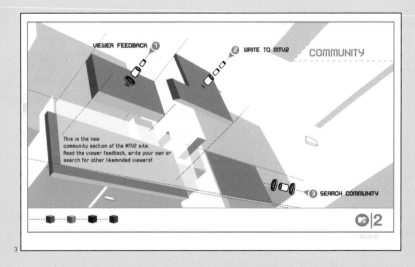

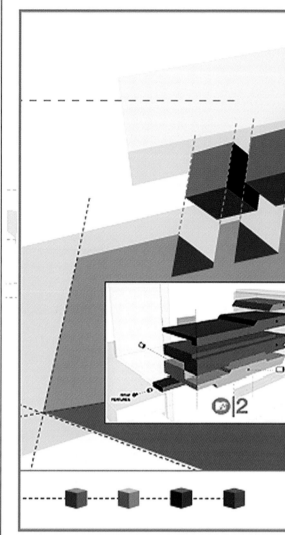

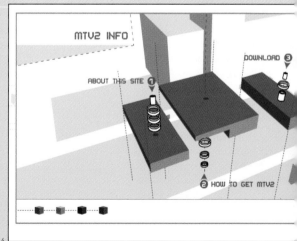

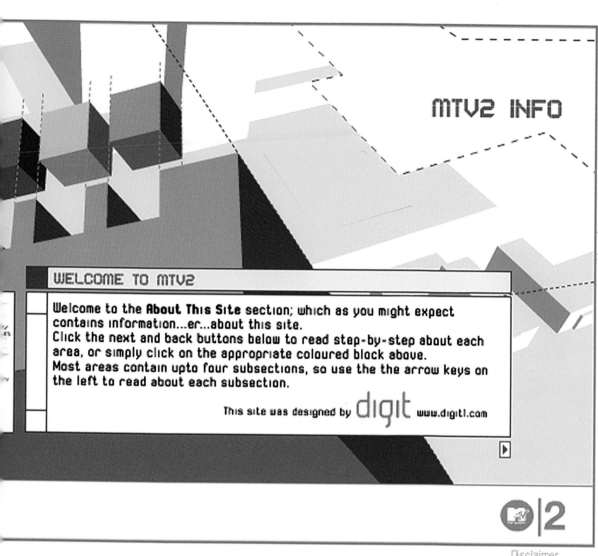

MTV2 INFO

WELCOME TO MTV2

Welcome to the **About This Site** section; which as you might expect contains information...er...about this site.

Click the next and back buttons below to read step-by-step about each area, or simply click on the appropriate coloured block above.

Most areas contain upto four subsections, so use the the arrow keys on the left to read about each subsection.

This site was designed by digit www.digit1.com

Disclaimer

1–4

The menu pages for each of the four sections of the website.

5

The site's main objective is to lay out information in a way that is easily accessible.

http://www.vcu.edu/artweb/CDE/index.htm

54

http://www.vcu.edu/artweb/CDE/index.htm
opening
http://www.vcu.edu/artweb/CDE/index.htm
OK

html>   Communications Art + Design
[script]

Virginia Commonwealth University
        School of the Arts

        [image : Enter Communication Arts + Design]

Enter   Communication Arts + Design

**Netscape 4.x or 6.0| Internet
Explorer 5.x recommended.**
        Optimally viewed at 832x624 resolution with
Verdana   font.
        [image : -]
        THIS SITE UPDATED AUGUST 2001
        [image : -]
        This site is maintained by
        Communication Arts + Design *webmaster*

325 North Harrison Street   Richmond VA
23284-2519   804-828-1709

http://www.has.vcu.edu/bis/forensic/index.html

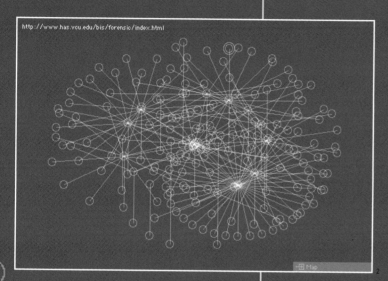

-꒰ Map

2

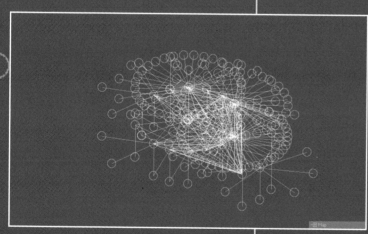

-꒰ Map

3

-꒰ Map

4

1–5
Web Stalker

Created by Escape (UK) in collaboration with Matthew Fuller, an independent software artist, Web Stalker is an experimental application that maps all the links related to a web session. Escape was formed by Simon Pope and Colin Green to evolve their successful interactive media design practice. Web Stalker consists of five primary functions – Crawler, Map, Stash, HTML Stream and Extract – that allow the user to gather and store links for future use.

Crawler connects Web Stalker to the World Wide Web and collects URL link data. After a URL has been entered, Stalker opens the internet connection and accesses the site. During Crawler's search of the site and its links, a dot moves across a bar that is divided into three areas to indicate Crawler's status [1]. The first section of the bar shows the progress of the net connection; the second follows Web Stalker as it reads through the HTML (HyperText Mark-up Language) document looking for links to other URLs; and the third monitors Web Stalker as it logs all the links.

Map visualizes HTML documents as circles and the links between them as lines [2–4]. Sites with the most links to them have brighter circles. When a web session has begun, the user can map it, starting with the first URL opened by Crawler and then moving through all the links from that site on to the links from the next sites. To see the URL of an HTML document, and its likely contents, the user clicks on a circle and the URL is displayed in the top left of the map window. Another circle appears inside the selected circle so that the user can keep track of the HTML document when moving from circle to circle.

Stash is a flexible way of saving URLs in a document format that records web use and can even be read by 'old-style' web browsers. Stash files can be passed around as separate documents between different users so that they can share information on web resources. HTML Stream displays the HTML as it is read by Web Stalker. Lastly, Extract [5] shows all the text from a URL or the user can read the text of an HTML document if a circle is dragged into the Extract window.

55

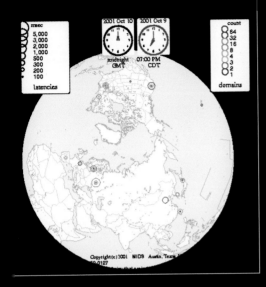

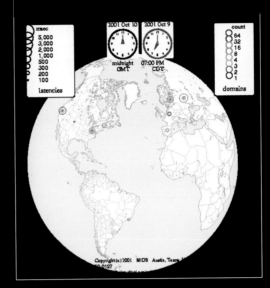

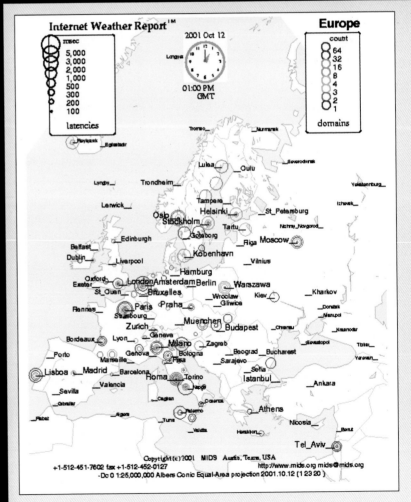

Internet Weather Report™ Europe

Internet Weather Report

Animated scans of conditions within the internet are laid out like newspaper or television weather reports. The IWR uses Java applets that allow non-stop viewing or single-step (frame-by-frame) views through GIF maps. The reports are presented as geographical maps that depict lag or latency,

the amount of time it takes to send a packet of data and to receive a response from an internet domain. The report is carried out every four hours, six times a day, seven days a week.

Latency is depicted by colour-coded circles. Small circles indicate good internet performance

(i.e., a fast link), while big circles denote problems in the internet. The colour corresponds with the number of hosts at a given location and latency, for example, red means only one host, orange is for two and green for nine. Violet signifies many hosts and occurs in densely packed areas like Silicon Valley.

The number of circles and colours change over time. A clock and text at the centre top of each map display the date, local time and time zone. Many of the maps span geographical regions, so multiple time zones are included.

The latency scale is measured in milliseconds

(one thousand are equivalent to one second and one hundred to a tenth of a second) and is calculated five times for each node, with the average shown. The average latencies for all the nodes for each scan make up the scan's geographic map.

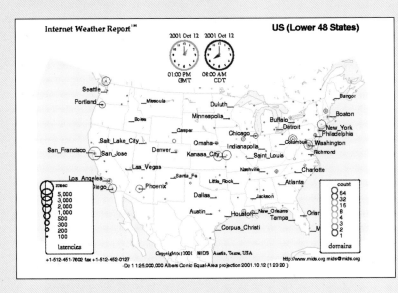

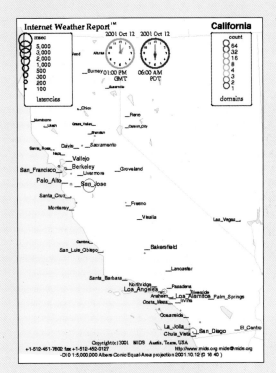

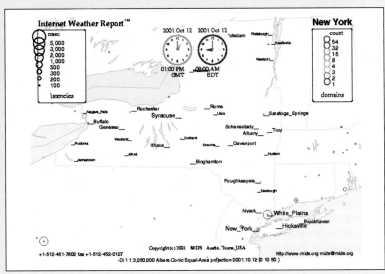

Informing

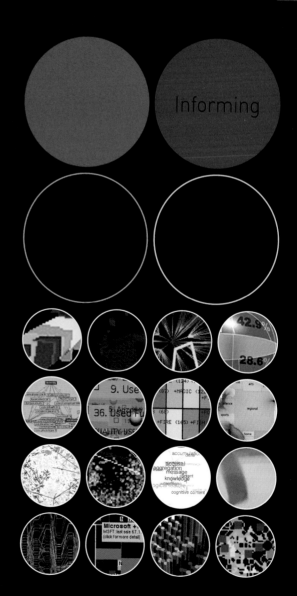

Informing

The analysis and presentation of data from such areas as communication, demographics and news.

Researchers and practitioners in the field of information visualization generally work with large bodies of scientific, financial or other commercial data. The root of information visualization is in graph drawing, the goal of which is to make data easier for human interpretation.

If the data elements have a structured relationship, visualization methods are used to represent the data elements (nodes) and their relationship with each other (edges). If the data elements do not have a structured relationship, the graphs are employed to discover and highlight any relationships. Graphs are used to illustrate hierarchical – structured – data found in everyday processes, projects and organizations, for example, files and folders on desktop computer operating systems, website maps and organizational charts that require relational layouts. The Cartesian grid, a network of parallel

lines intersecting at right angles on a two-dimensional plane, is one system that can accommodate unstructured data in such layouts as bar graphs, line graphs and scatter plots. Visually, graphs use colour, line, shape, texture, symbols and icons within a defined context to aid the perception and understanding of the displayed information.

As the cost of computer hardware falls, the number of display devices multiplies and the abilities of computer software increase, it has become possible to tap into bodies of information on a daily basis, for instance, news stories, the stock market, bank accounts, music and movie collections, purchasing histories and medical records. The dramatic growth of the World Wide Web in the public realm since 1990 has resulted in a strong demand for ways of sifting through, editing and making sense of the huge information stores. Access to information

gives individuals power – the power of knowledge and understanding and the power to take action. However, the growth in a computer's processing ability does not necessarily mean that we have greater access to information. It simply allows more information to accumulate and overload our senses.

Advances in computer processing and display technologies have further disconnected human and machine in terms of intelligent communication. The computer recognizes words by their binary system, a sequence of zeros and ones. It is only capable of collecting, synthesizing, storing and transmitting the zeros and ones as raw data, which is meaningless until structured into information. Consider an internet search-engine query for information on the name 'Saluki'. The computer understands the word as a sequence of numbers, not for its meaning: 'any of an ancient breed of tall, slender, dog developed in Arabia and Egypt and having a smooth, silky, variously coloured coat'. The challenge is to build into computer processors the ability to discern the semantic and pragmatic elements of the

word in the same way as humans use spoken and written language.

Whereas 'Mapping' features projections of spaces, this chapter presents visualizations of bodies of information and raw data, qualitative and quantitative, and which are not necessarily physical entities or structurally related. 'Informing' looks at internet search queries, web crawlers and mechanisms that are initiated with a human action and go on to produce results. As with 'Mapping', there is no standard method, but the challenges addressed in this section are more specific. What is the best way of visually presenting daily news information? How can we access our financial accounts from our computer desktop, mobile telephone or PDA? How can major stock exchanges monitor the performance of stocks and the systems that display the information and send the results to us? How can we make sense of the findings from an internet search query? More fundamentally, how can the computer understand a word's semantic and pragmatic qualities in addition to its syntactic properties?

New York Stock Exchange
Architectural design group Asymptote turned the floor of the New York Stock Exchange into a 3-D virtual environment. The 3-D trading floor is used by operators as a real-time support system for computer networks and information flows. Visitors to the datascape are literally part of the environment.

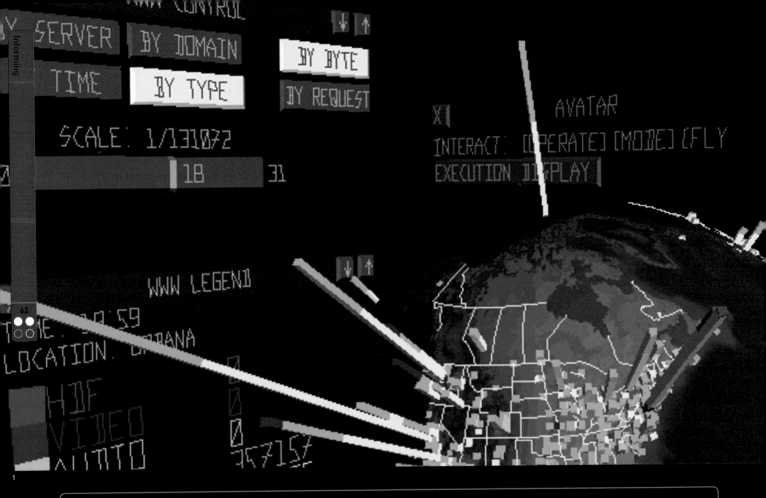

1–3
Web Traffic Skyscrapers

Due to the explosive growth of the World Wide Web, studying patterns of web traffic is an important first step in designing future generations of internet servers that can accommodate new media types and interactive elements. Daniel Reed and his colleagues from the Pablo Research Group at the University of Illinois, Urbana-Champaign, US, have developed a system to do just that.

Avatar, a virtual reality system, examines and displays real-time performance data and compiles an analysis of web traffic. It offers an insight into the presentation of data and allows the quick creation of new display metaphors. Three different metaphors are used: time tunnels, scattercubes and geographic displays. Time tunnels analyze timelines and event-driven graphs of task interactions. Scattercubes, 3-D views of 2-D scatter-plot graphs, provide an understanding of multidimensional, non-grid-based, time-varying data. In the virtual environment, one can fly through the projections to explore the data space, rescale the axes and activate or disable the history ribbons. A 3-D global perspective is used for a summary view and a simple flat projection for local observations. Data can be displayed as either arcs or bars between the source and destination, with thickness, height and colour denoting specific attributes. Each bar is placed at the geographic origin of a request. The bar's colour bands represent the distribution of document types, domain classes, servers or time intervals between successive requests. The most valuable aspect of the geographic display is its real-time nature – one can easily study temporal variations and see the day-by-day effects of evolving document trees, new service providers and changing network topology and bandwidth.

1 Menus offer interaction with the display of World Wide Web data. Sliders control the size of the globe and the height of the bars. The globe can be rotated at various speeds and a pull-down menu provides the option of 'warping' to a particular location, i.e., North America or Europe.

2 Data is portrayed on these two maps of the globe as stacked bars, which convey information through their position, height and colour. Bar heights show location-specific attributes, such as the number of bytes or the number of requests relative to other sites.

3 This diagram shows a 3-D projection of the National Center for Supercomputing Applications (NCSA) server. Three axes correspond to the number of data bytes transferred for video-clip requests, the number of bytes transferred for text requests and the number of requests.

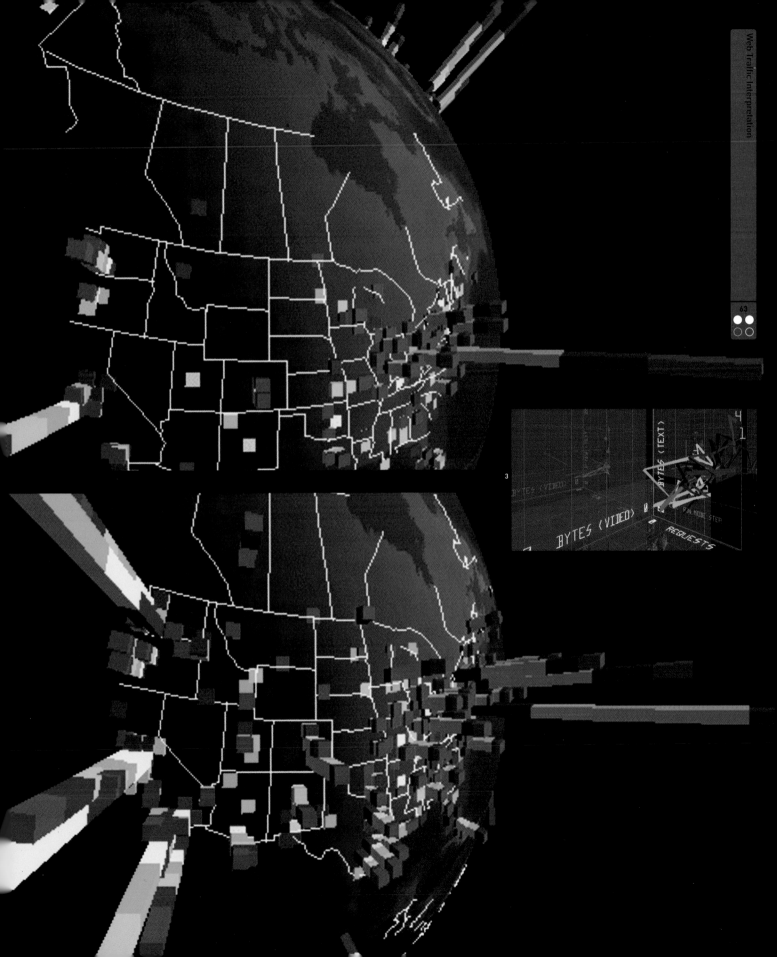

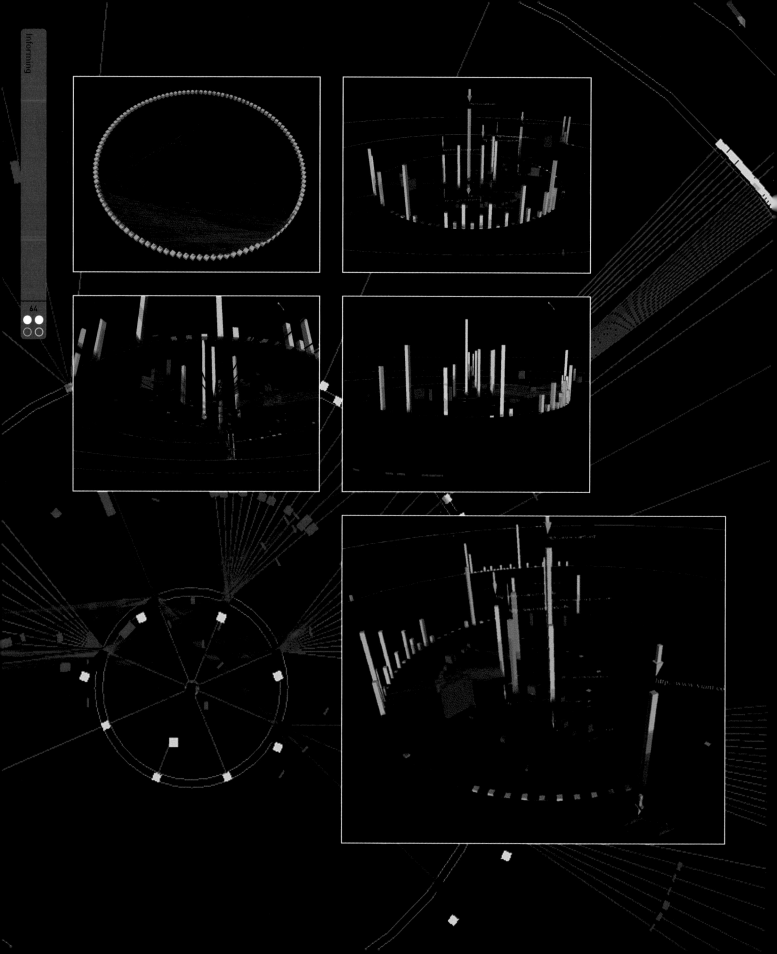

64

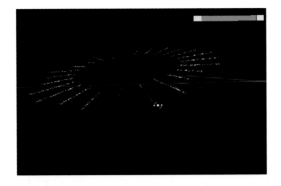

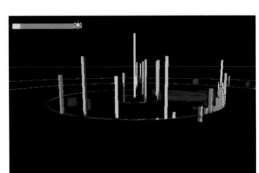

Web Traffic Project

Led by Antoine Visonneau and colleagues at the Center for Design Informatics (a research unit at Harvard University Graduate School of Design, US), the Web Traffic project develops 3-D visualizations of online behaviour using VRML. Work began with a series of experiments that highlighted the connectivity between a database and a 3-D environment. The researchers see great potential in 3-D immersive environments and believe that in the future people will come to work, meet and interact in information spaces or information landscapes.

The project involves a series of 3-D structures that build on one another. First, a radial structure of red bars and 3-D typography is constructed. The webpage name appears beside a bar whose length is determined by the number of people who visit the page.

The second stage of the project tracks how many people go between pages or the number of times a connection is used. The pages, represented by 3-D bars, are arranged in a circle, with red lines indicating the connection between pages.

The final stage merges what was learned from the previous stages to organize the website in a more advanced radial structure. Bars stand for pages; their size shows the number of hits the page has received. On mouseover the name of the page appears next to green or yellow arrows that show entry and exit pages. The size of the arrow is directly proportionate to its rank.

The next stage could include such categories as male and female activity, providing even more comprehensive data.

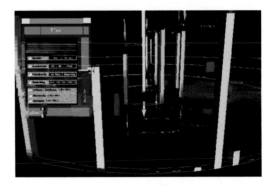

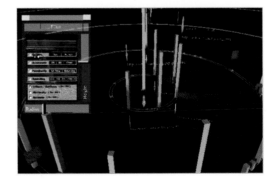

Spreadsheet for Visualization

Command:

Picking....value=dt970416c pt=4172 pos=-100 3.89414e-005 -25
Document ID = 4172 = docs/news.html has 2113
Picking....value=dt970416c pt=3387 pos=-76.6044 64.2788 -25
Document ID = 3387 = docs/Investor/Contents.html has 1208

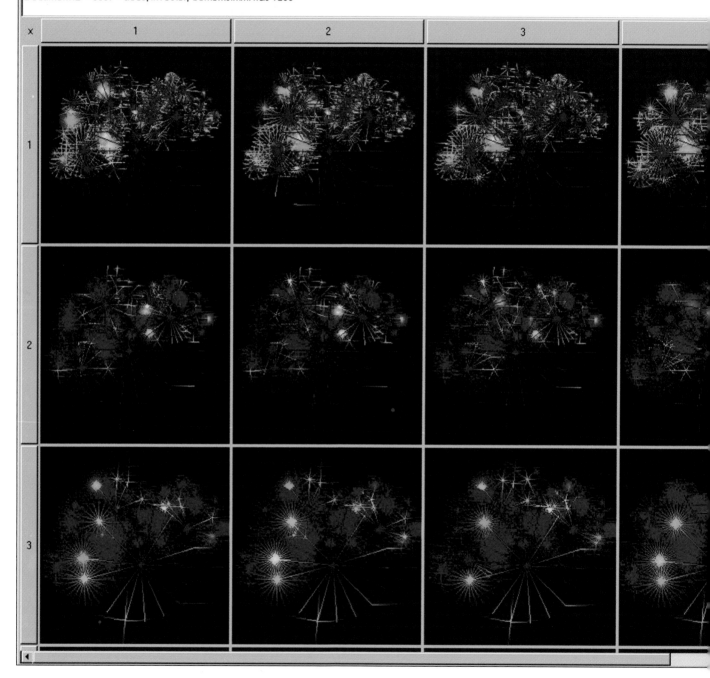

Visualizing Spreadsheets

Ed Chi and Stuart Card of the Xerox Palo Alto Research Center, US, have focused their research on sense-making. They have introduced a concept that uses the spreadsheet layout with cells containing visualizations of complex data. The example presented here concerns the research centre's huge, 15,000-file website, parc.xerox.com. The spreadsheet layout provides a structured, intuitive and powerful interface for exploratory data analysis, based on three elements:

1) The grid. The tabular layout allows users to view collections of visualizations simultaneously.
2) Operators. These generate or modify cell content and can be applied across entire columns or rows.
3) Dependency. The spreadsheet keeps track of the dependencies between cells, updating them automatically when they are manipulated. These examples are Disk Tree visualizations –

a layout that centres around a 2-D circle – with the larger image indicating how Disk Trees discover the more popular areas of the website. The colours reveal patterns and trends in the relationship between content usage and topology. Each cell represents a week of visitor activity on the website. The smaller image is constructed by subtracting one usage pattern from another to make sense of the different areas visited on the website.

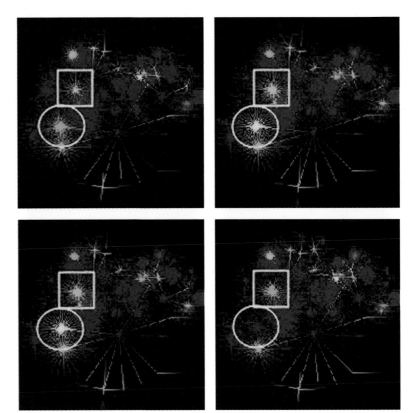

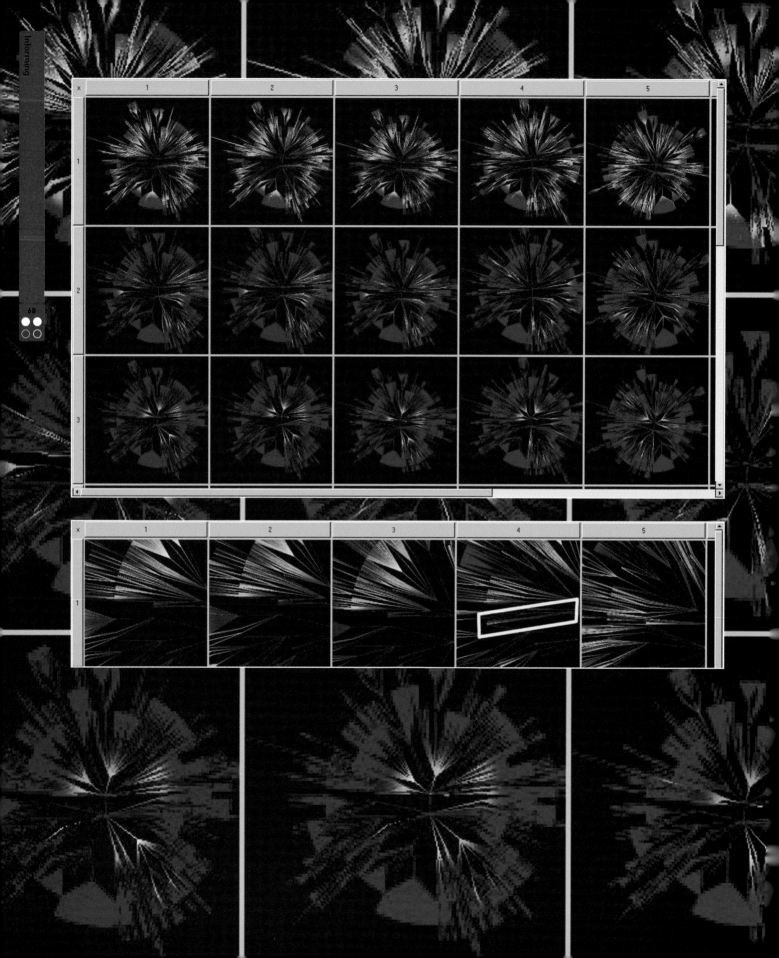

Datascapes
The Presentation and Assessment of Complex Information

The word 'asymptote' is defined as two parallel lines continually approaching and virtually merging at the vanishing point at an infinite distance from their origin. Asymptote is also an architectural design and research practice established by architects Lise Anne Couture and Hani Rashid in New York in 1989. Asymptote's projects range from spatial experimentation to building and urban design and from installations to computer-generated architecture. The studio's work examines the influence of present-day cultural practices and technologies on architectural space and design. Technological intervention, particularly digital technologies and our new spatial relationship to information, has encouraged Asymptote

to explore and transform the traditional architectural concerns of enclosure, form and order.

Concept Asymptote created these models for Richard Saul Wurman's TEDX Conference and for his book *Understanding USA*. Each datascape model answers a question or set of questions about a specific demographic in the US, such as employment status and race or city growth rate and earnings. The datascapes attempt to transcend conventional graphing and charting systems with new methods of reading, gathering, recording and visualizing data, thereby offering a more thorough understanding of information.

American Demographics
This datascape combines all the subject-specific datascapes to create an overview of demographics in the US.

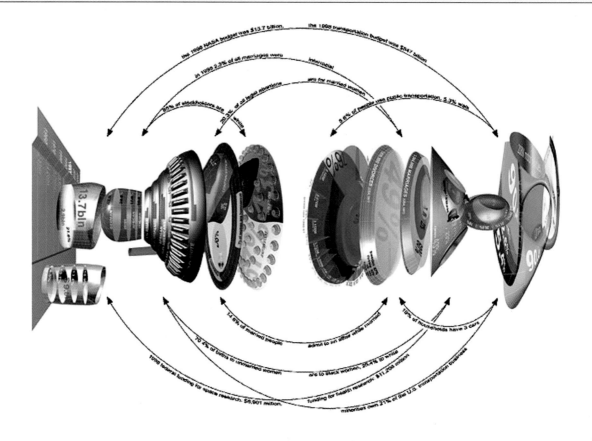

Structure Datascapes are interactive entities for porting through the internet. Initially, they were rudimentary wireframe structures in Maya software and were kept lightweight to allow them to be read efficiently despite the bandwidth restrictions of the internet as it exists today. Completely updatable, the models are resident in a virtual space that can be infinitely scaled and transformed.

Context Each data structure is organic, more specifically biomorphic, with such surface characteristics as light and shade. Externally, the datascapes appear as malleable containers of information that grow and change as new data is incorporated – effectively a living record of all past, present and future data inputs.

Navigation The structures on these pages are presented as VRML (Virtual Reality Markup Language) models that are accessible and navigable on the internet. Information can be explored in a variety of ways. Each 3-D model can be manipulated, allowing different views, perspectives and readings. By choosing one element of the datascape and adjusting it according to a specific set of criteria, other related items can also be reconfigured. Various correlations can be made with data that might otherwise be invisible or misinterpreted.

Datascapes Sequence
A developmental sequence of eight of the datascape models illustrates how each is constructed.

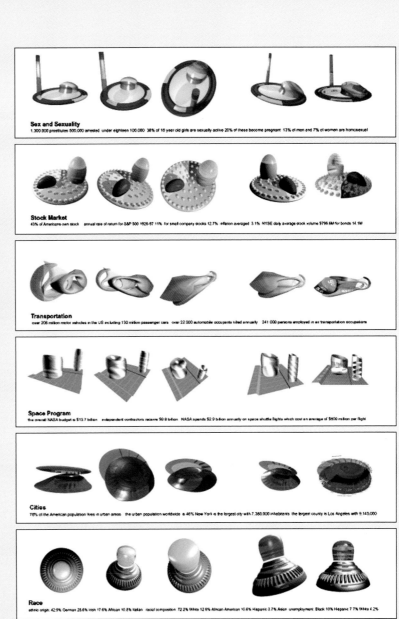
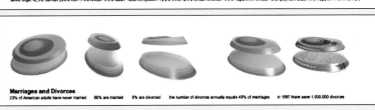

Sex and Sexuality

Stock Market

Transportation

Space Program

Cities

Race

Marriages and Divorces

Families

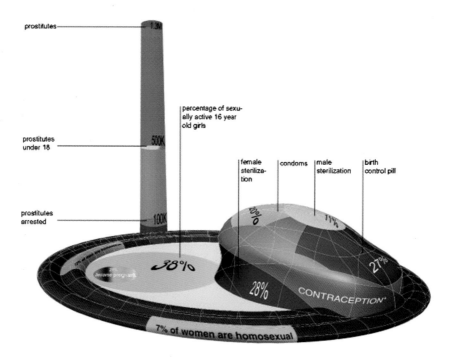

Sex and Sexuality
What contraception
methods are being used?
Who is sexually active?

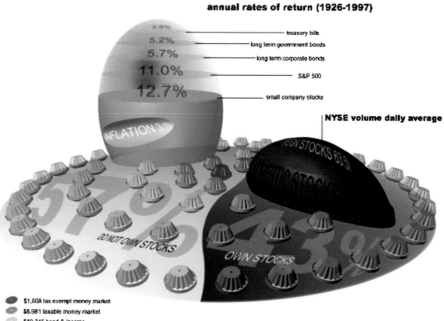

Stock Market
How many Americans invest
in stocks and what kind of
stocks do they prefer?

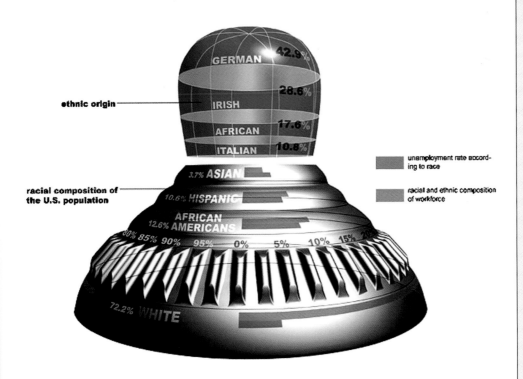

ethnic origin

racial composition of
the U.S. population

GERMAN 42.9%

28.6%

IRISH

17.6%

AFRICAN

ITALIAN 10.8%

3.7% ASIAN

10.6% HISPANIC

12.6% AFRICAN AMERICANS

80% 85% 90% 95% 0% 5% 10% 15% 20%

72.2% WHITE

unemployment rate accord-
ing to race

racial and ethnic composition
of workforce

Race
What percentage of
Americans is represented
by each race? What is the
employment status of
each race?

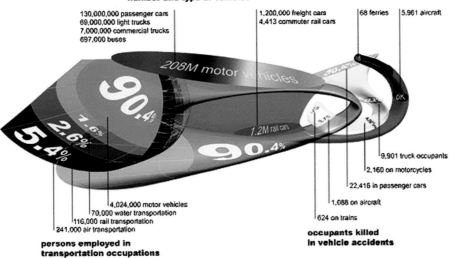

persons employed in transportation occupations
number and type of vehicles
occupants killed in vehicle accidents

number and type of vehicles

130,000,000 passenger cars
69,000,000 light trucks
7,000,000 commercial trucks
697,000 buses

1,200,000 freight cars
4,413 commuter rail cars

68 ferries

5,961 aircraft

208M motor vehicles

90.4%

1.6%

2.6%

5.4%

1.2M rail car

90.4%

3.1%

6K

9,901 truck occupants

2,160 on motorcycles

22,416 in passenger cars

1,088 on aircraft

624 on trains

4,024,000 motor vehicles
70,000 water transportation
116,000 rail transportation
241,000 air transportation

**persons employed in
transportation occupations**

**occupants killed
in vehicle accidents**

Transportation
This datascape reveals
how Americans move
between places.

SQWID

Developed by Scott McCrickard, Colleen Kehoe and Amy Opalak at the Georgia Institute of Technology, US, SQWID (Search Query Weighted Information Display) is a Java-based tool for visualizing search results from World Wide Web queries. SQWID is especially useful for analyzing broad searches that yield a large number of results because it wades through all the information to form a graph based on the frequency with which key words feature. Terms that are closely related to the query appear as nodes on the graph. The relevant sites are arranged in a triangle formation. Sites that closely correspond to the key terms are situated near to the nodes, while sites that are not so clearly linked to the terms are further away from the nodes. Sites that lie in the middle of the triangle are applicable to more than one term. Using the menus and sliders, the user can control the number and date range of sites, break sites into pages and view the links between sites.

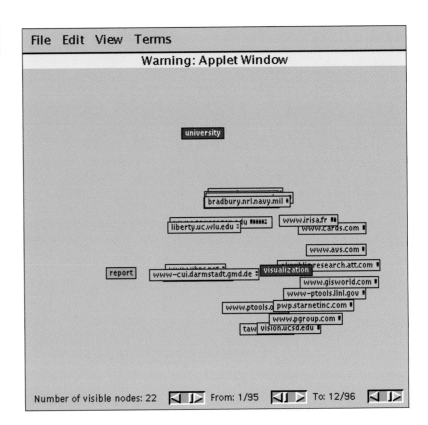

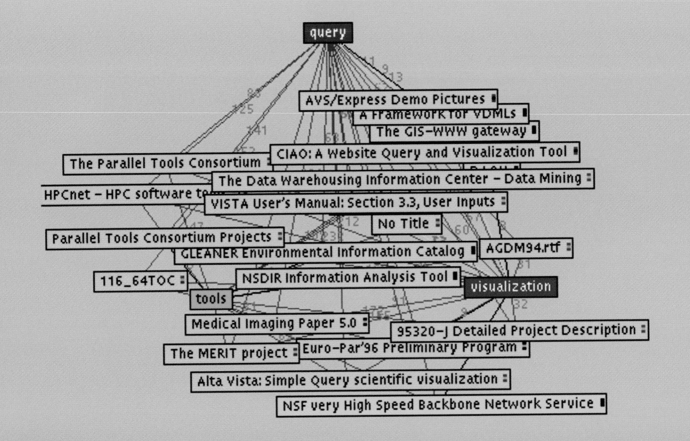

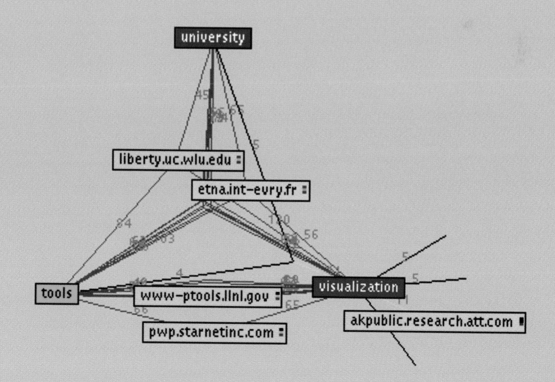

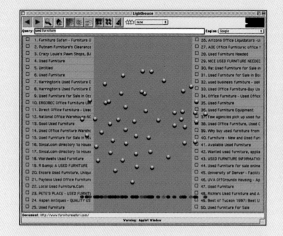

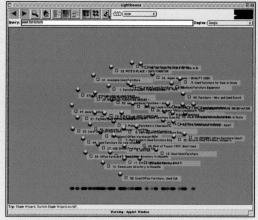

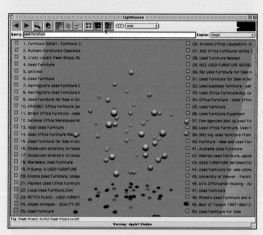

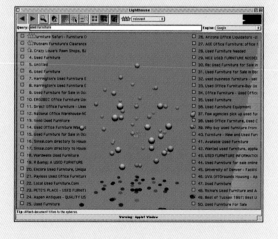

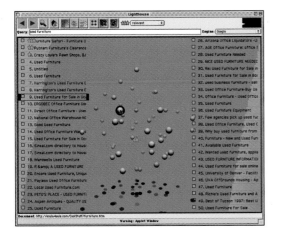

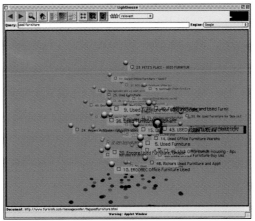

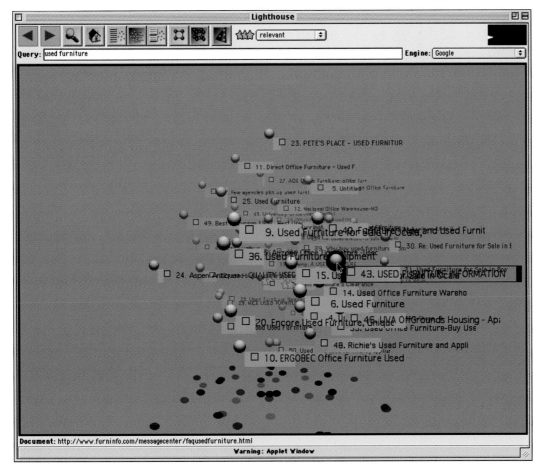

Lighthouse

An interface concept for information retrieval, Lighthouse was developed by Anton Leuski and James Allan from the Center for Intelligent Information Retrieval at the Department of Computer Science, University of Massachusetts at Amherst, US. The project combines a traditional ranked list with clusters of documents, and also incorporates a 'wizard' to help users to navigate the material.

The format is determined by selecting one of ten search engines from which to retrieve information, including Excite, Yahoo! and Google. The user also chooses such settings as the maximum number of documents to be found and decides on one of four retrieval methods. The images show the results of a search for used furniture.

Other features show the query as an object and use colour gradients and patterns to exhibit hierarchies or categories. Toolbar commands range from the standard forward and backward instructions to commands that rank, visualize or cluster titles, showing the results in 2-D or 3-D.

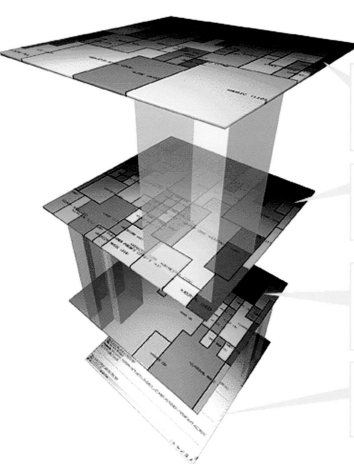

The top-level map shows forty odd broad entertainment 'subject regions' represented by regularly shaped tiles. Each tile is a visual summary of a group of Web pages with similar content.

When a user selects the 'MUSIC' subject region, a second-level map with numerous different music categories is then presented to the user.

Delving deeper, the user wants to learn more about jazz music, so clicking on the 'JAZZ' tile leads to a third-level map, a fine-grained map of jazz related Web pages.

Finally, selecting the MILES DAVIS' subject region leads to more a conventional looking ranking of pages from which the user selects one to download.

ET Map

In 1995, Hsinchun Chen of the Artificial Intelligence Laboratory at the University of Arizona, US, developed the ET Map as a method of visually grouping the seemingly endless websites that are listed upon an internet search. The image here charts a large part of the entertainment section of Yahoo!, with some 110,000 different web links. To find information of interest, the map can be browsed and questions asked using the familiar point-and-click navigation.

Kohonen, an artificial intelligence (AI) technique, produces a self-organizing map (SOM) that uses a neutral network approach typically associated with the automatic analysis and classification of a text document's semantic content. Web content is categorized to match human perception.

ET Map uses one important, but common-sense, spatial concept in its organization and representation on the web: the land plat metaphor. The size of the 'subject region' is directly related to the number of webpages in that category. Subject regions with closely related content are plotted near to each other. The map also has different layers that show a finer degree of categorization.

The top-level map, roughly forty tiles, represents very broad areas of entertainment, such as magazines, music and beer. The figure in brackets indicates the number of webpages in that category. Select one of these options and a second-level map appears with a more detailed breakdown of one of the first areas. For example, pick 'music' in the first instance and the next level's tiles show different types of music. Choose 'classical' and the third-level map offers a wide choice of related names or pieces. The layout of the fourth-level map is in a more familiar format, listing relevant websites.

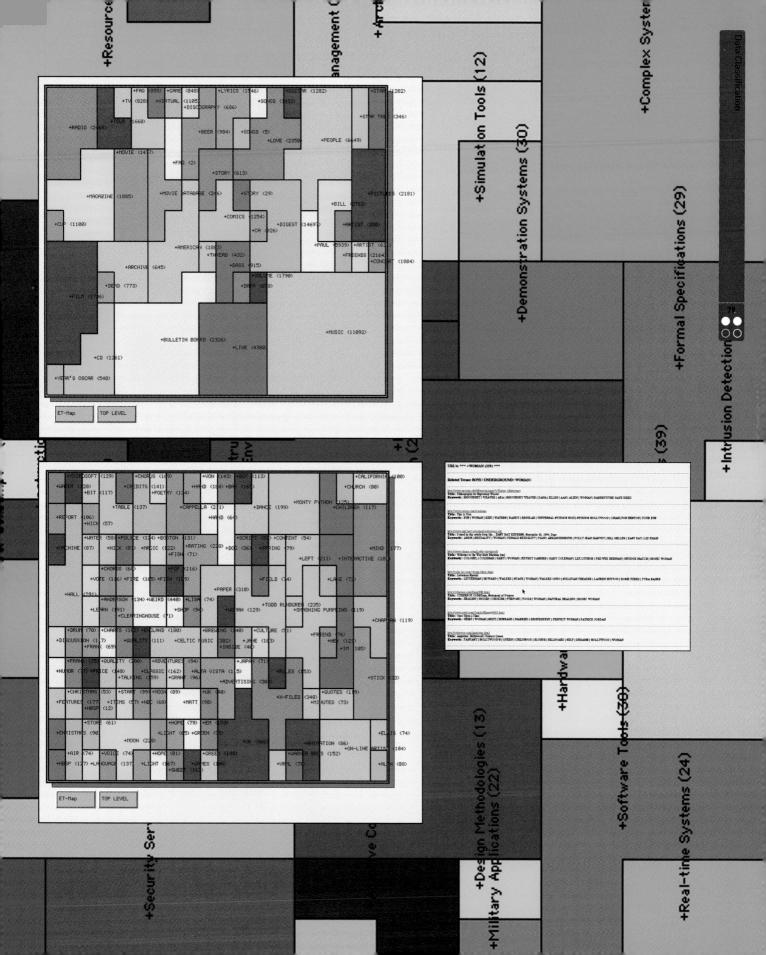

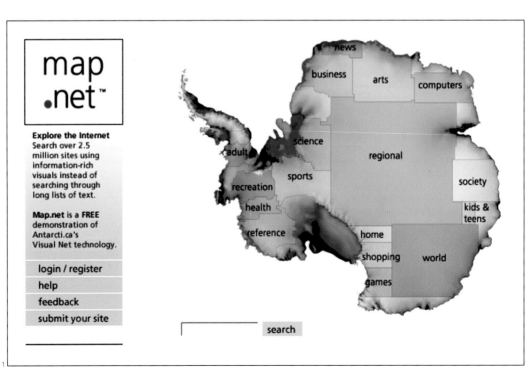

80

map.net™

search ● everywhere ○ this map

start   map   filter   landmarks   teleport   chat   help

You are here

What am I looking at?
outgoing links
incoming links
pages on site
this site is cool

tell me more

email this map
feedback
about us
set home page

powered by visual net™

© 1999 – 2001 Antarctica Systems Inc. All Rights Reserved

Categories:
Start / Arts /

Subcategories:
Animation
Architecture
Art History
Bodyart
Celebrities
Classical Studies
Comics
Crafts
Design
Digital
Directories
Education
Entertainment
Genres
Graphic Design
Humanities
Illustration
Literature
Magazines and E-zines
Movies
Music
Online Writing
Performing Arts
Periods and Movements
Photography
Radio
Television

Animation
Celebrities
Crafts   Design
Comics   Genres   Illustration
Bodyart   Education
Architecture
Art History   Classical Studies   Dave's ESL Cafe
Garfield's Official Web Site   ArtLex - dictionary of visual art

Harmony Central Main Menu

Music

Literature   Movies

StarWars.com

Performing Arts   Photography   Television   Visual Arts
Radio
PhotoLinks   Researchpaper.com
PlayBill Online Chats   Writers Resources
Inkspot: The Writer's Resource
The Perseus Project

10 of 238047 sites shown

Help build the largest human-edited directory on the web

map

---

map.net™

Explore the Internet
Search over 2.5 million sites using information-rich visuals instead of searching through long lists of text.

Map.net is a FREE demonstration of Antarcti.ca's Visual Net technology.

login / register
help
feedback
submit your site

news
business   arts
computers
science
adult   regional
sports   society
recreation
health   kids & teens
reference   home
shopping   world
games

search

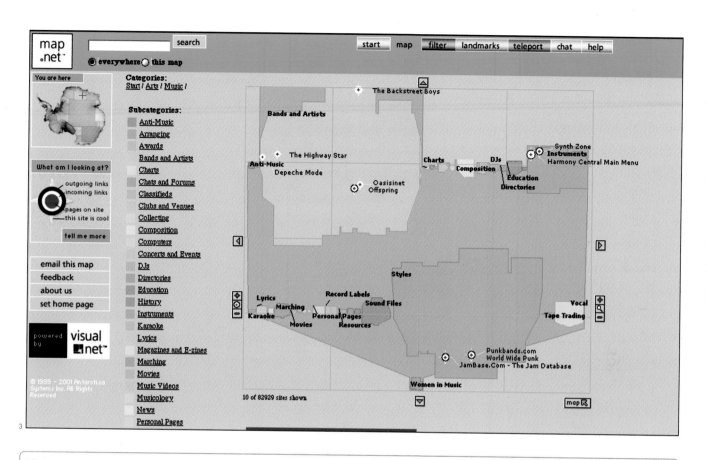

1–3
Map.net

Visual Net™, developed by Antarti.ca, is a new way of viewing, organizing and searching for data, transforming it into visual maps and enabling users to see all relevant and related information.

Map.net is constructed using Visual Net. It has been divided into such categories as home, science, arts, health and world [1]. Click on a category and a new map of that particular region appears, again broken down into smaller categories. Select another category and the process repeats itself. This is similar to a map of a country that is split into provinces or counties and then divided into cities and neighbourhoods. The subcategories are arranged alphabetically in rows from left to right and top to bottom. For example, selecting 'art' from the first map takes the user to that section's subcategories: photography, visual arts, music, comics and body art [2]. By choosing one of these, the process repeats itself, so 'music' breaks down into such areas as record labels, DJs, instruments and women in music [3].

As the maps on Map.net are explored, the category legend to the left of the map keeps the user informed and can be used to navigate the subcategories. The category path sits above the legend and serves two functions: to inform the user of the path taken to arrive at the current map, and to allow immediate access to any upper-level category.

On the map, web links are portrayed as 'targets' and once hit the particular website is opened in a new window. Each of the rings on the target provides information about individual websites, although not all targets have rings. The thickness of the black ring shows how many links the site has to other websites. When searching for general information, a site with many links is a good starting point. A white ring portrays the number of other sites that have links to this one. Experience suggests that this is a valuable indicator of a site's popularity. The size of the red dots represents how many pages are found on the site. Yellow Arrows signify that the ODP (open directory project) editor has declared the site 'cool'. There is no substitute for human judgment, so a visit to the sites would be beneficial.

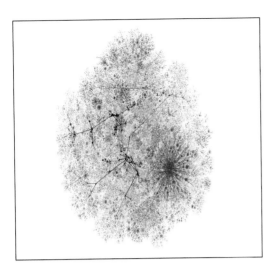

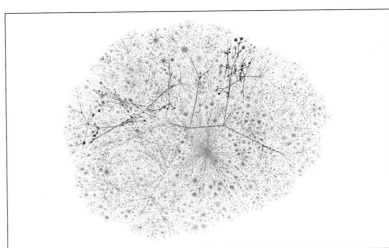

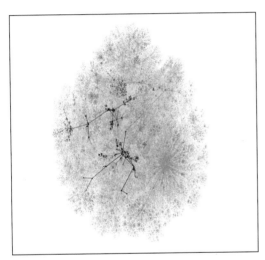

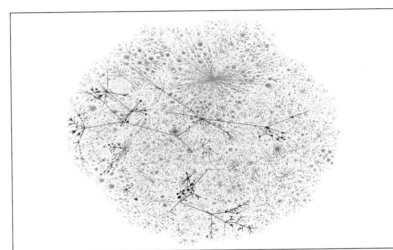

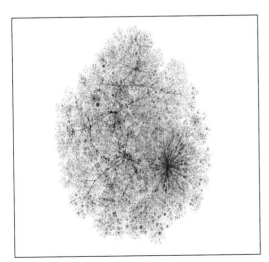

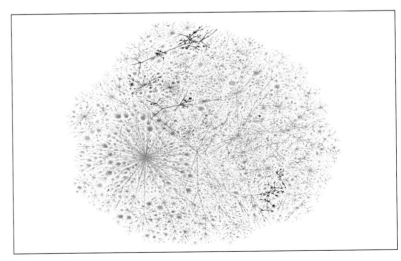

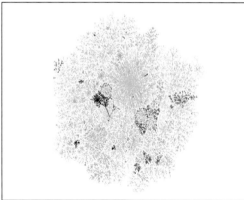

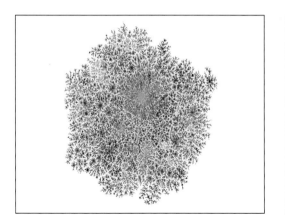

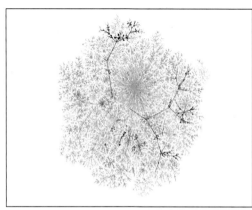

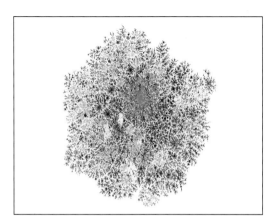

Internet Mapping Project

Developed by Hal Burch of CMU (Carnegie Mellow University, Pittsburgh, Pennsylvania, US) and Bill Cheswick of Bell Laboratories, the Internet Mapping Project collects and visualizes routing data on the internet. This long-term project consists of frequent traceroute-style path probes, one to each internet service provider. From this information, trees are built showing paths to most of the networks on the internet. This process is useful for gaining a better understanding of large networks and extranet connections.

The net-mapping program sends small UDP packets to random ports with a lot of links. Each packet's time-to-live (TTL) field is set differently and is reduced on leaving a port. When it hits zero, a packet's death is reported back to the sender. If a packet fails to return, perhaps because it was lost or dropped by a firewall, a couple more attempts are made and the return code is noted.

A treelike map of the routing data displays more than 65,000 end points and thousands of internet interconnection nodes. The colour scheme is based on the IP (Internet Protocol) address of the nodes thus showing communities that share similar network addresses.

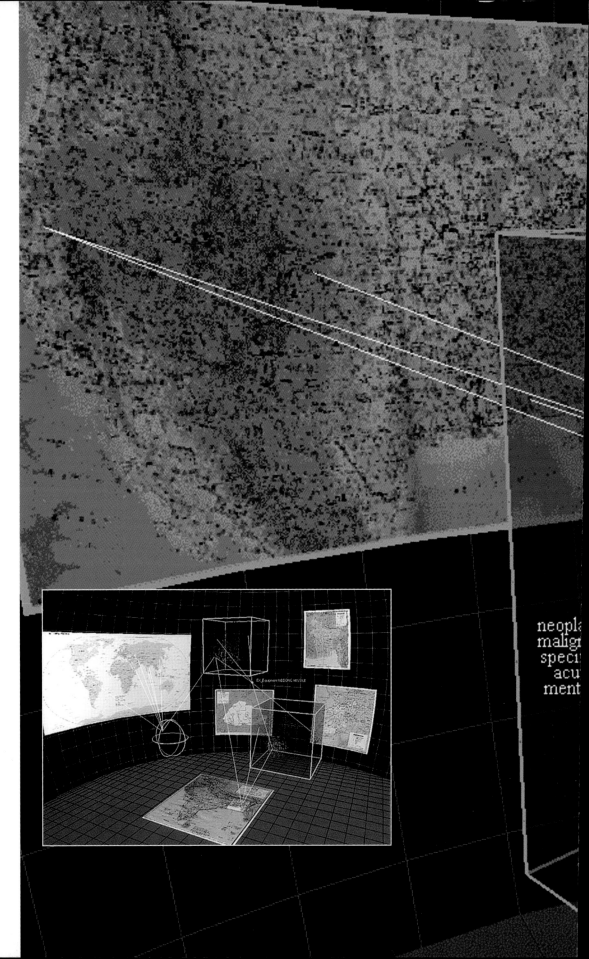

Starlight

In today's hectic world of information overload, we have access to electronic and digital data, maps, video and satellite imagery. How do we make sense of it all?

Developed by John Risch and researchers at the Pacific Northwest National Laboratory, US, Starlight software is an immersive 3-D environment that displays and analyzes complex multimedia data. Originally created for US intelligence, Starlight produces a 3-D image based on a user search. A cluster of data points is contained in a 3-D cube, with links to the source. In the images presented here, the source is a geographic map.

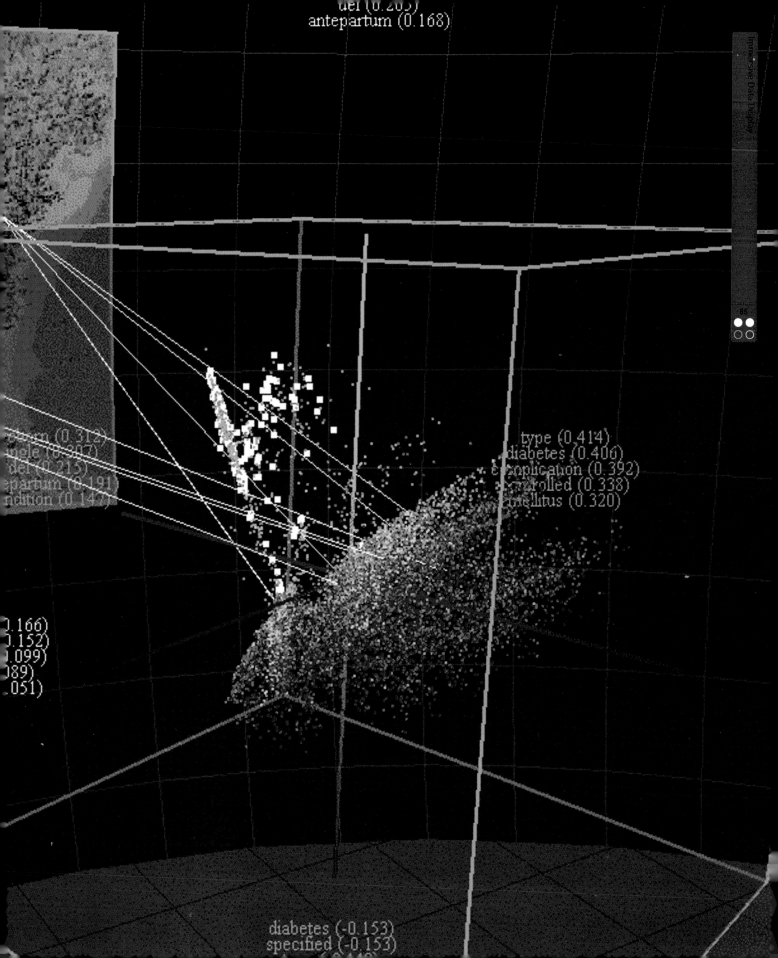

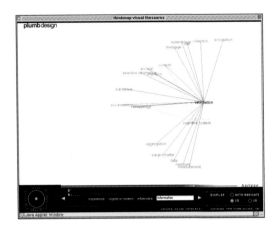

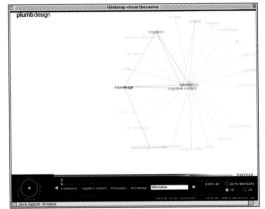

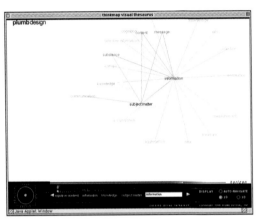

Thinkmap

Thinkmap Inc. manufactures software for displaying, animating and navigating complicated and interconnected information. Its Java-based developer solutions, such as Thinkmap Studio and Thinkmap Application Server, are the foundation for creating innovative applications and services. This new generation of complex, data-intensive knowledge-management and e-commerce systems has led to custom-made, interactive interfaces that are intuitive and 'human-centric'.

Plumb Design Visual Thesaurus was developed as a demonstration of Thinkmap's ability and is linked to the WordNet database set up by the Cognitive Science Laboratory at Princeton University, US. Thinkmap shows the various meanings of words and their relationship with other similar words in the English language. The WordNet database, first created in 1985 as a dictionary based on psycholinguistic theories, contains over 50,000 words and 40,000 phrases with

more than 70,000 meanings.
The structure uses an arc-node configuration, with nodes represented by words and arcs illustrating the sense relationship between words. Tones of grey are used to highlight words, and provide a sense of depth in the overall appearance. Presented with this structure spinning and turning in space, the visitor must click on a specific word to summon more words from the database, thus creating a web of linguistic relationships.

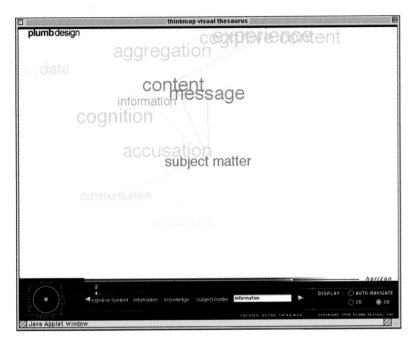

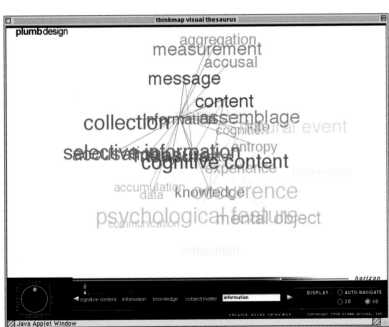

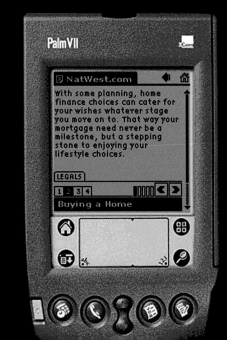

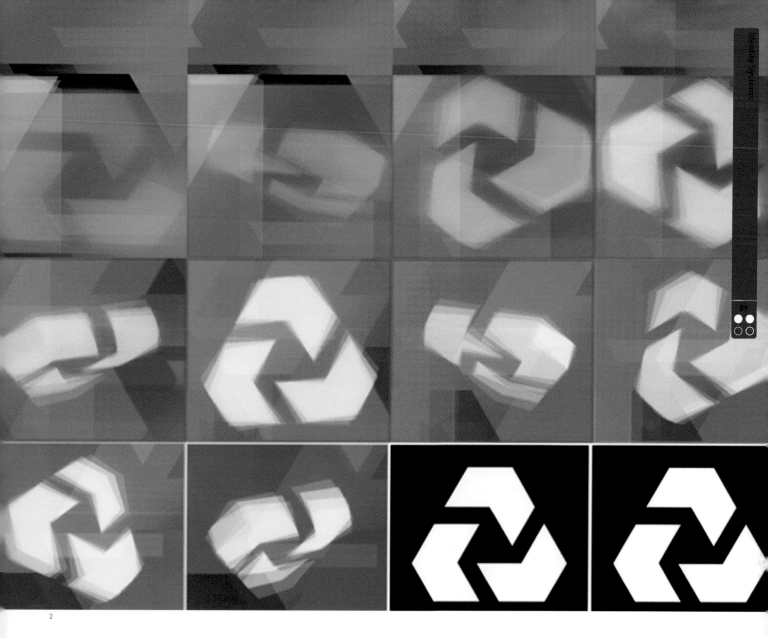

2

3

Media Neutral

The term 'media neutral' describes the one-off creation of a body of information that is structured to work on any transmission device, be it a website [2], e-mail, mobile telephone [3], ATM machine or PDA (personal digital assistant, 1). Thomas Müller and Razorfish are leaders in this new field of communication design.

Here, Müller was challenged to adapt the NatWest.com identity system to several transmission formats: ATM machine, PDA and mobile telephone. In each case, the identity system had to be applied appropriately to the medium's resolution and the availability of time.

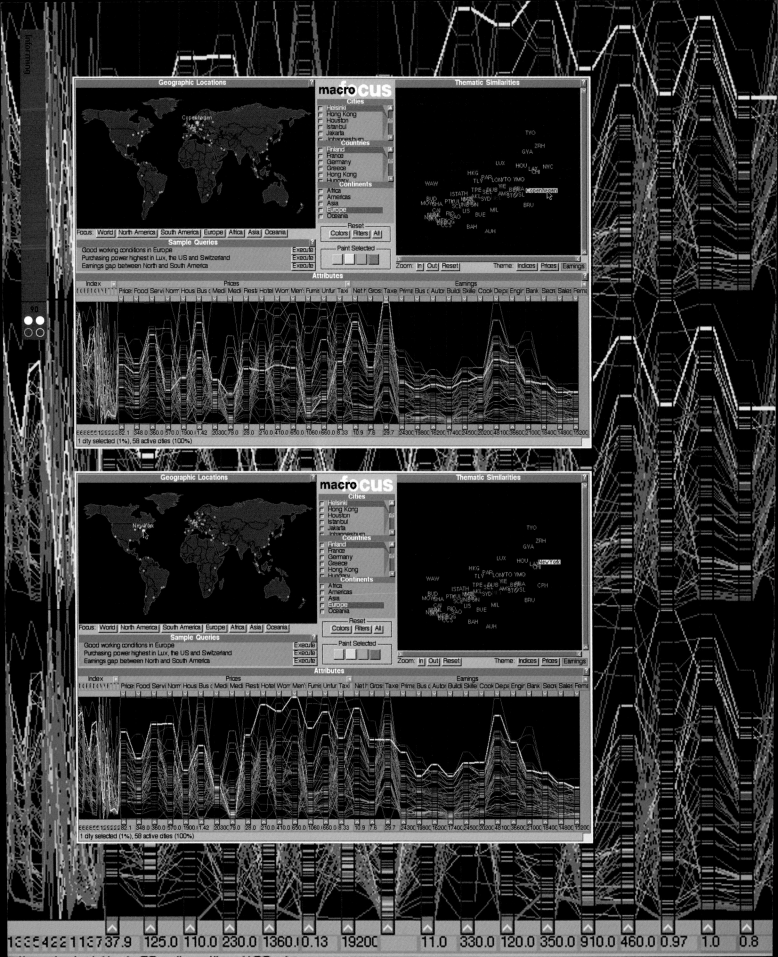

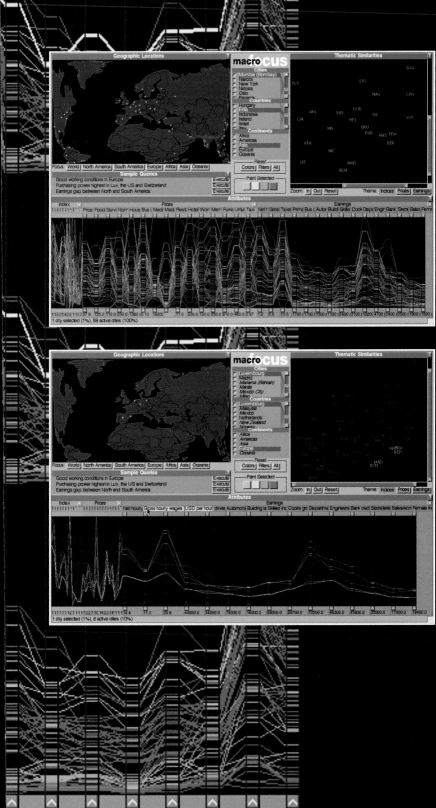

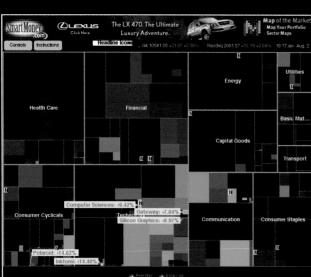

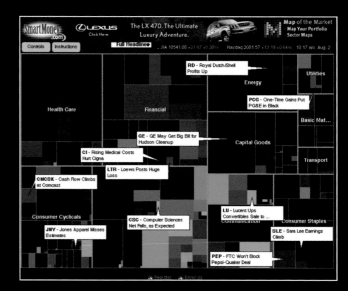

Map of the Market

Developed by lead information designer at SmartMoney.com Martin Wattenberg and launched in 1998, Map of the Market is a tool for spotting investment trends and opportunities. It maps the stock performance of more than five hundred companies simultaneously, with data updated every fifteen minutes.

Map of the Market is a tree map, with each coloured rectangle representing a different company. The size of the rectangle indicates the company's market capitalization (the larger the tile, the greater the value of the company) and the colour shows price performance. Green means the stock price is up, red means it is

down and black suggests it is stationary. The denser the colour, the bigger the change in the stock's value.

Moving the mouse over a company's rectangular tile activates a window offering more information, and clicking on a particular firm brings up a menu. The menu's first two options concentrate on a specific

sector or industry, while other items take the user to SmartMoney's interactive research tools for news, detailed financial data and historical graphs.

Companies are grouped in eleven sectors and within these by industry. Within each industry, neighbouring companies have a similar history in their stock price movements, allowing

the map to reveal regularities in market movement and to showcase trends.

Furthermore, the user can view other time periods, change the green and red colour combination to blue and yellow in consideration of colour-blind users, highlight the top five gainers or losers, or find a particular stock.

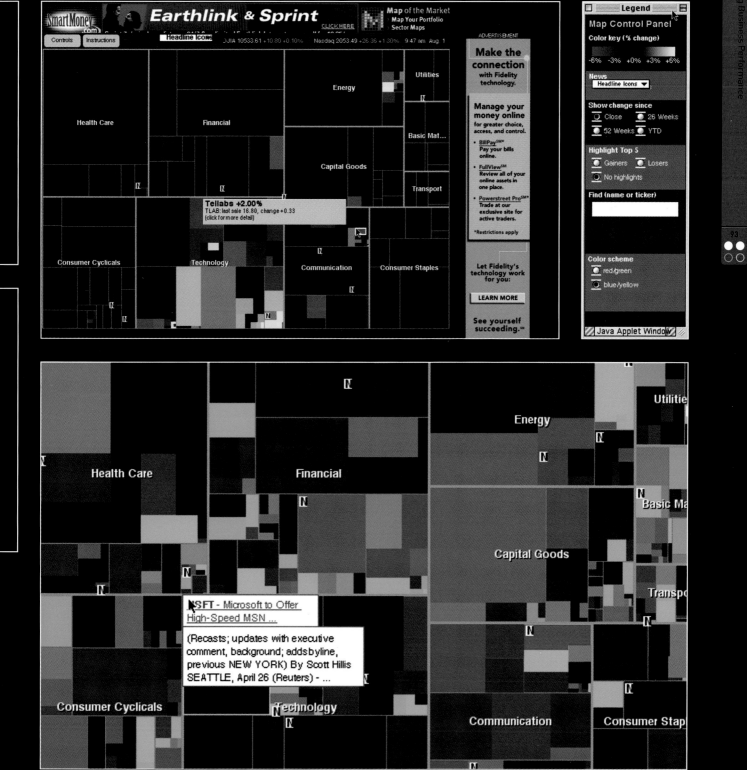

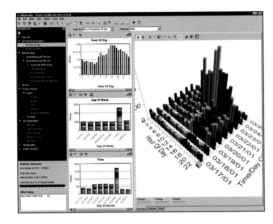

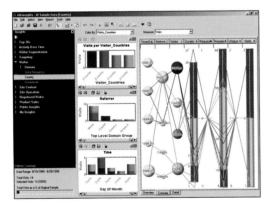

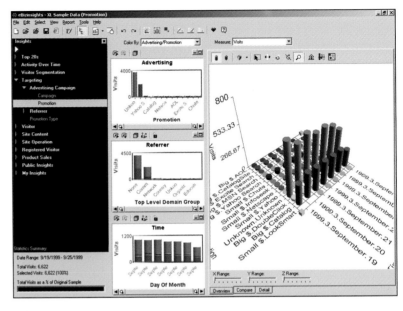

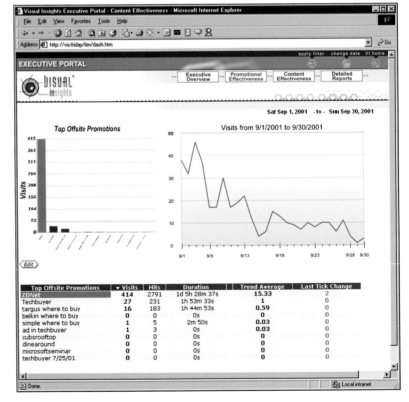

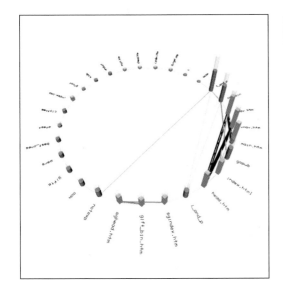

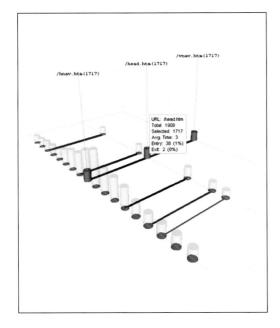

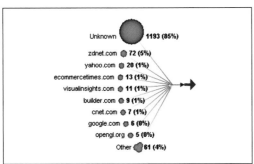

eBizinsights

A multifunctional software application developed by Stephen Eick and powered by Visual Insights' Visual Discovery and realTime 3-D technologies, eBizinsights is an ebusiness performance-management and web-analysis tool that provides immediate and accurate comprehension of site performance and activity, visitor behaviour patterns and promotional effectiveness. eBizinsights is built upon the premise that in the fast-paced, competitive world of ebusiness the best opportunities are hard to spot. Static, summary-level graphs generated by first-generation, web-reporting tools often fail to provide sufficient information, while waiting for hours (and often days) to receive reports from IT departments can result in missed chances.

The patented Visual Discovery gains an insight into complex relationships by creating interactive visual displays to help the user identify trends, make comparisons and find hidden connections among business dimensions. By mapping information as visual metaphors, Visual Discovery simplifies the display of complex multidimensional relationships and facilitates decision-making. RealTime 3-D allows users to monitor activity as it occurs, and Visual Path Analysis enables effective site design and marketing.

Interactive visuals feature exploratory, ad-hoc and 'what-if' analyses. Drill-down capabilities (highly focused searches into a specific area deep in the website infrastructure) eliminate fumbling with the interface, encouraging the user to 'interact' with the data in an intuitive manner and to reach a new, deeper level of understanding.

The structure and form of eBizinsights is highly customized, with such features as 'scalability' (an industry buzzword describing the flexible and expandable abilities of a software application), which accounts for a company's growth. Visual scalability allows the user to compare hundreds of elements, providing insights far beyond the 'top 10 reports' of first-generation solutions. The user can define business dimensions for comparison and reporting, and can analyze promotions, commerce types and visitor patterns. The software's extensible architecture enables users to insert data to maintain a unified view of their business as it grows.

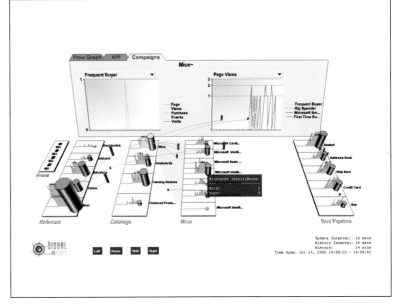

NicheWorks + Exploratory Data Visualizer (EDV)
Conveying Information about Large Networks

CASE STUDY

Concept The difference between displaying networks with 100 to 1,000 nodes and those with 10,000 to 1,000,000 nodes is not merely quantitative; according to Graham Wills at Bell Laboratories, it is also qualitative. The density of nodes and edges (links, or the relationships between nodes) displayed per inch of computer screen requires special visual techniques to display the graphs and focus attention. Compounding the problem are the large real-life networks, often weighted graphs that have additional data associated with the nodes and edges.

Structure NicheWorks is a visualization tool for the investigation of very large graphs and specifically portrays graph structure and node and edge attributes so that patterns and information hidden in the data can be seen.

NicheWorks has been applied to many real-life domains; telephony, software analysis, e-mail patterns, information retrieval, website analysis and medical data. Originally a stand-alone tool, it is now part of the EDV (Exploratory Data Visualizer) environment, also developed at Bell Laboratories. EDV is a suite of tools that generates a number of data views, connected by data linking that allows interesting facets of the data in one view to be highlighted in other views. This way, intricate dependencies can be explored without creating over-complicated visuals.

Context Capable of rapid graph layout, NicheWorks can be used on a good PC on graphs with up to 100,000 nodes; on more powerful work stations, the figure could rise to millions of nodes and edges. The tool offers multiple layout methods and display options so that various types of information and tasks can be supported.

Navigation Colour, shape, size and position convey information about data associated with the links and nodes of a network. The user can adjust the display to identify and focus on clusters of interesting nodes. By selecting a set of nodes or links with a given characteristic from a statistical plot, the same nodes will be highlighted in a graph view.

Visualizing Patterns in Hardware Store Receipts

This case examines over 1.8-million receipts taken from a group of hardware stores over the course of a week. For each item sold, its cost, department and class was recorded, with each receipt stating what was bought, how many and at what price. Discount information was also noted. With this information, Wills constructed a NicheWorks data set by linking items based on their probability of appearing on the same receipt. The placement algorithm in NicheWorks then grouped the items into clusters and placed them close to other items they are often purchased with.

1

1

A node's colour and shape indicate its department and its link colour and size determine the strength of its association with another item.

2–4

Wills zooms in to explore an 'island' that looks like a combination of two different product types that are often bought at the same time. Close inspection reveals that most items in the island come from two departments, which tend to get bought mainly with items from their own department. This raises a few questions: what are the two main departments, what are the single items from the other departments (represented by single green circles), what is the item from the 'red triangle' department that is more often bought with items from other departments than with items from its own department?

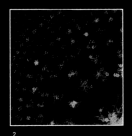

2

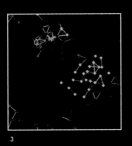

3

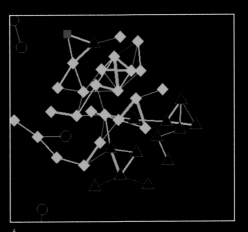

4

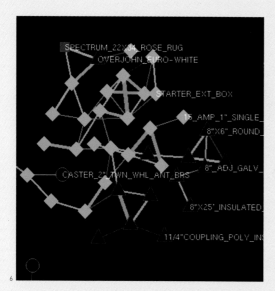

6

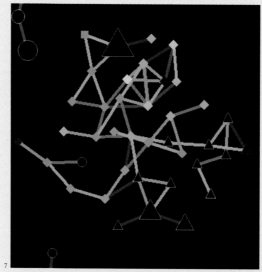

7

5

The two main departments
are labelled electrical and
plumbing. A reasonable
guess might be that this
island represents a common
set of purchases by
contractors building or
redeveloping houses.

7

After establishing what the
island represents, the data
can be explored in more
depth. Wills changes the
nodes' colours to depict sales
in dollars – blue is low, red is
high – and maps the nodes'
sizes to the average
percentage discount.
The node shape still
stands for its department.
This reveals that electrical
components are not subject
to discounts, but that some
of the plumbing items,
in particular the toilet
bowl, have fairly high
reductions.

6

A short description of the
items reveals that most of
the plumbing purchases
are types of piping and
the electrical products are
extension boxes and cabling.
The single occurrence of an
item from the building-
material department is a
rug, which is often bought at
the same time as a toilet seat
from the plumbing section.

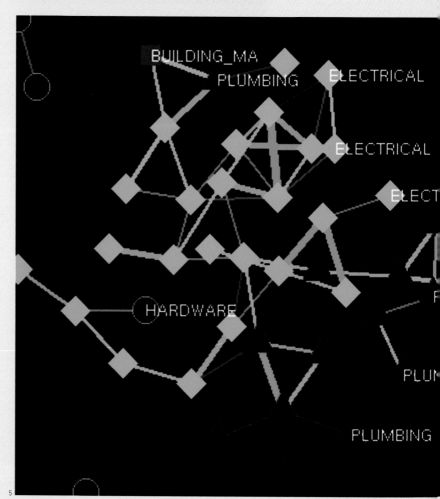

5

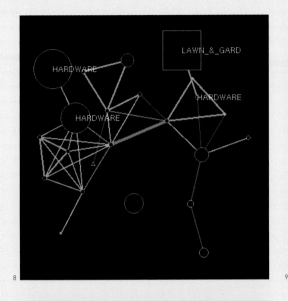

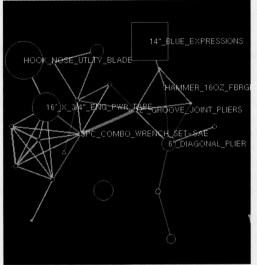

Shown are two related, heavily discounted hardware items – tape and a blade. It seems most probable that people buy the blade to cut the tape than it does they buy the tape to go with the blade. In fact, the tape is connected to a set of items that are bought together quite frequently, whereas the blade's only tie is to the tape.

10

A search for expensive items in another data view comes up with a piece of lawn and garden equipment (lower right). A common pattern of buying discounted hardware items also appears (top left). There is an extremely strong link between an item in plumbing and one in hardware, as shown by the thick red line.

11

The expensive item, a 14-horsepower tractor, has generated a small cluster of items it needs to run well. The strongest link (indicated by a thick red line) is between a screw and a particular screwdriver.

12

An overview of the data set.

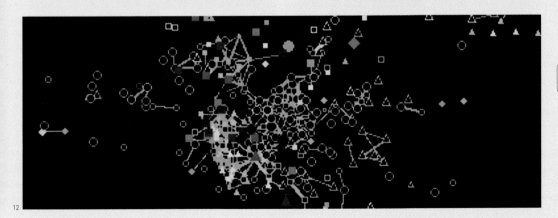

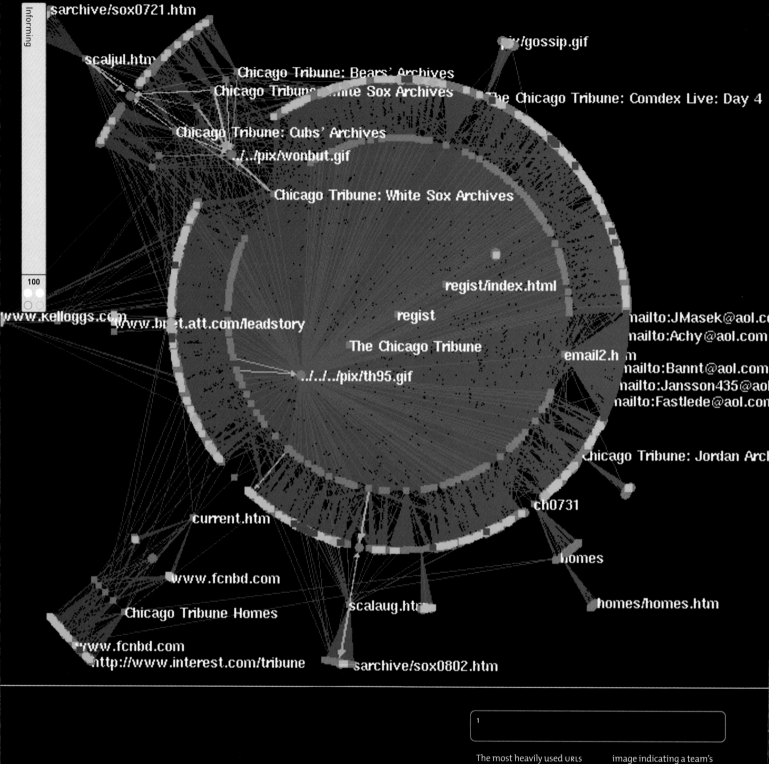

The most heavily used URLS
are the Tribune banner
(pix/th95.gif, inside the
centre circle) and an

image indicating a team's
victory (pix/wonbut.gif,
upper left outside the
large circle).

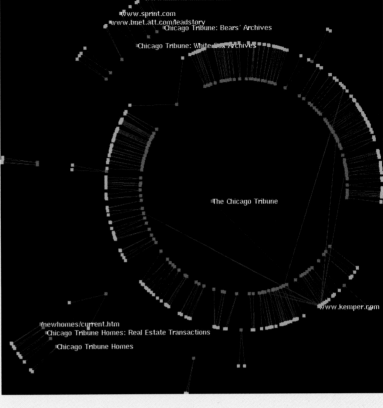

Project Title: The Chicago Tribune

The Chicago Tribune is one of the two most important Chicago newspapers and is a good example of a well-structured, commercially oriented website. The site made its data available for investigation, and the examples here have been explored using NicheWorks. The goal was to understand the site's structure and to find what design criteria had been used in its production.

First, the links were gathered and the nodes categorized within the site. No links or mail-to functions that led away from the site were included. The site was laid out using the tree method and a coding system shows the type and status of the nodes: orange squares are local pages, orange circles represent local images and blue squares stand for off-site pages. Visitors cannot go off-site without reading at least one other page, a common feature of commercial webpages.

2

This image is the result of searching for all the URLs that include 'AdID' and selecting all the links to those pages.

3

Seen from the same position as the first overview, this view serves as a good comparison point.

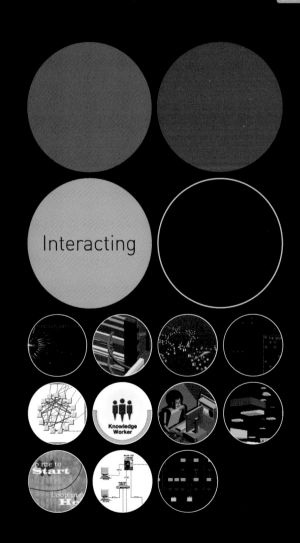

Interacting

Interacting

Visualizing a complex event, action or process, such as a conversation between two or more people or between human and computer. Devices include internet chatrooms and gameplay.

The terms 'interaction' and 'interface' are often used synonymously. However, the two are very different. Interface – the key part being 'face' – is defined as a surface forming a common boundary between two regions or bodies. It is the point or method of communication between a user and an inanimate object (such as a computer or household appliance) or the communication between a computer and another inanimate device (such as a printer). A keyboard and mouse are physical interface devices for humans to input information into the computer and to use software. Windows, icons, menus and pointers are digital interface devices within a computer operating system that assist humans in using the computer efficiently and effectively. Most interface actions are explicit – 'yes', 'no', 'off', 'on', 'fast', 'slow' – and pertain to the operation of something.

Interacting – the key element being 'act' – demands a much deeper involvement with the computer. It is a more ambiguous process that incorporates the shifts and changes that occur in a complex event or action, such as a conversation between two or more individuals. Interaction can take place face to face with people sharing the same physical space and time, or it can take place between two or more individuals in different places and at different times. This type of communication requires a mediation device. There have been many through history: post, telegram, printing press, telegraph, telephone, fax machine, pager and, the most common today, the computer.

Websites are not simply about interfaces. For many, the web is a rich and dynamic environment in which to interact with individuals, groups and information, a place where it becomes possible to

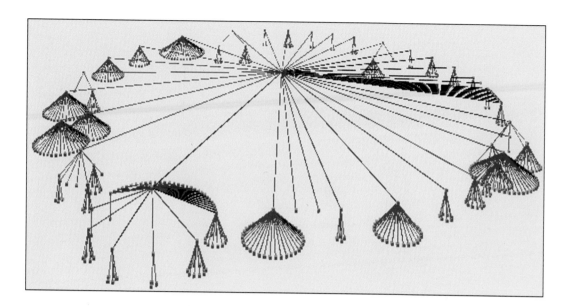

interact directly with the computer itself. Consider searching and browsing. An example of the former is a search-engine query, where the user enters one or several key words. It can be an open search engine, such as Google or Yahoo, or a closed engine, such as a specific library-holdings catalogue. Whatever the system type, a search requires input and produces output. There is no control over what the engine collects in its search, though limitations can be imposed by users with a knowledge of formalized query languages. Nevertheless, searching is mainly an automated input or output procedure with the help of the computer. The user has more control when browsing and is involved during the actual search process, with the computer putting choices to the user: Should I take this road or that road? Should I take this link within this website, or should I take this route to another website? The user actively participates and is in charge of searching, sifting, editing and directing pathways and information.

Other types of interaction include communication between individuals and groups in internet chatrooms, for example, in Usenet newsgroups the computer serves as a mediation device. This chapter presents research and development in this and other areas of online interaction. One area of research involves the concept of the avatar, a visual representation of an individual in a virtual environment, such as an online role-playing game. Avatars usually take on cartoonlike syntax and can have a real-life appearance or a more fictional look. There are limitations: most avatars are mere shells of the real individuals and they do not change over time or based on a user's interaction.

The challenge is to reduce an action or interaction into a simple visual representation without distortion or a misleading outcome. Methods of presentation vary from illustrations with icon systems and other pictorial elements to more abstract and symbolic approaches. All attempt to answer the questions: How does this specific process work? What happens during the process? How does one represent oneself on the internet? How many people are involved in this conversation? Who are the most and least knowledgeable?

Populated Information Terrain (PIT)
A virtual-reality database system, developed at the University of Nottingham, UK, PIT allows users to interact with information and to collaborate with each other in a digital environment. The bibliographic database shown here is virtually inhabited by users who are visible to one another.

PeopleGarden

Rebecca Xiong has developed visualizations of conversations in internet chatrooms as part of her graduate research at the MIT Media Lab, US. Many online interactive environments have a large number of visitors and it is difficult for users, especially new ones, to form a clear mental image of the people with whom they are communicating. How can information about these users be conveyed compactly between them?

Unlike a photographic portrait, which displays the physical characteristics (gender, age, race) of an individual, the data portrait is an abstract representation of a user's interaction history. Xiong has created the visual metaphor of a single flower – a PeopleFlower – to represent each data portrait. A garden of flowers combine the portraits to produce an online environment or conversational garden (PeopleGarden). Only information that is publicly available about each individual is used in the portrait.

The organic nature of the flower supports the idea of growth and change over time. Three pieces of information are shown in the petals: the time the message was posted, the number of responses and whether a post starts a new conversation. The time of posting is indicated in the petals' ordering and colour saturation; the more intense the saturation, the more recent the message. The number of petals increase as more messages are posted, similar to the blooming of a flower. Older petals move to the left as new petals grow on the right, maintaining a symmetrical shape.

Each PeopleFlower also displays the amount of feedback on a posting, a key element in illustrating interaction among groups of users. Responses are signified by pistil-like circles above the petals.

PeopleGarden can be used in other online environments to depict their social context and infrastructure. This is a valuable method of bringing online interaction closer to the benefits of physical interaction, but without the need for proximity or physical contact.

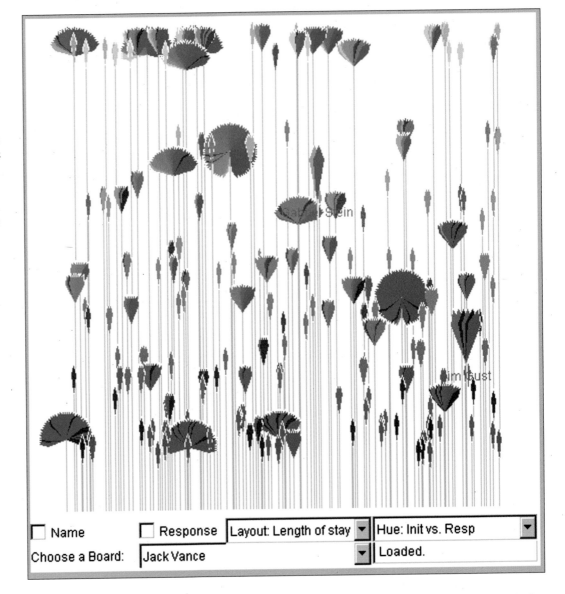

WebFan

WebFan is also based around the fact that web users have little knowledge about the activities of their fellow users, being unable to see the flow of online crowds or to identify centres of online activity. This tool can enhance a user's experience by visualizing the activities of others, answering questions about overall patterns and more specific queries, such as what are other people looking at, what is hot and who is interested in what I am interested in?

WebFan visualizes the messages and responses posted by users on web boards and creates a fan-shaped structure based on the replies. A hierarchical display method, WebFan shows a large set of webpages with many levels at the same time for overview and comparison. Each line stemming from the fan's base stands for a message, and the lines that branch off these indicate responses to the message. Users are represented by different colours and when a user reads a message, the line changes to the colour of the user. When multiple users read a message, the line becomes multicoloured. The user's location is marked by a circle.

Users move the cursor over the line to reveal more details about a message, such as title, author and date; clicking the right mouse button displays the actual message. The rolling lines under the 'Users' column on the right side of the visualization become triangles when they are highlighted. A triangle represents different user sessions, with the point of the triangle signifying the user's first visit to the web board and the base line of the triangle showing when the user leaves.

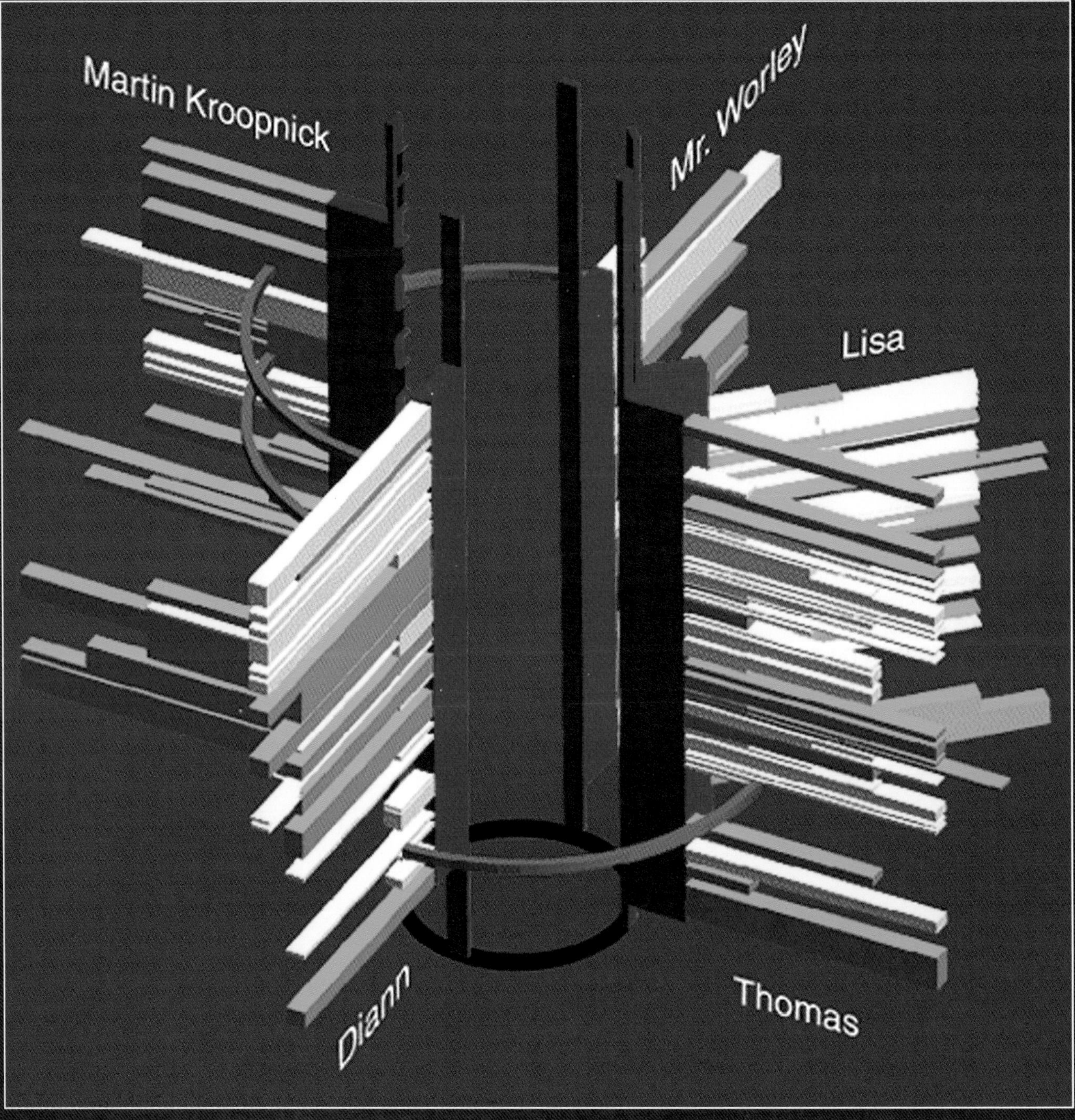
Martin Kroopnick
Mr. Worley
Lisa
Thomas
Diann

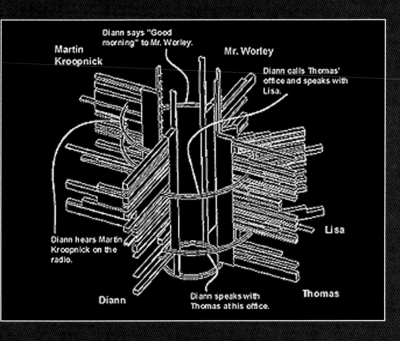

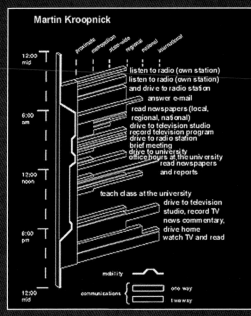

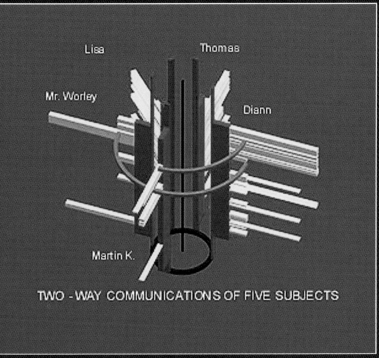

TWO - WAY COMMUNICATIONS OF FIVE SUBJECTS

Human Extensibility

Paul Adams researches ways to track personal communication within an organization to discover how social power and communication are related. One method uses Vellum, a CAD (computer-aided design) application, to model people's connections through time and space during the course of an ordinary day. The CAD models are stored as a set of objects in a database and can be rotated and examined from various angles.

The images illustrate the communication between five colleagues. Each communication is mapped on a vertical axis, which is divided into four parts that span a six-hour period of the day. Extending from this axis is a series of 3-D bars similar to those on a traditional bar graph. Each bar represents a one-way communication (radio, television) or a two-way activity (telephone, classroom). The display can be changed to show the various types of communication. The length of each bar is determined by the reach of the communication taking place, shown along a horizontal axis: 'proximate' is a communication that is taking place in the immediate setting, such as an office or classroom, while 'international' has the longest reach.

The overall structure resembles a turnstile display rack. Arcs can trace a circumference around the central axis and connect any two colleagues to highlight a specific communication. Yellow signifies a two-way communication, cyan depicts a one-way communication, magenta represents the time axis and light purple indicates a communication link between two colleagues.

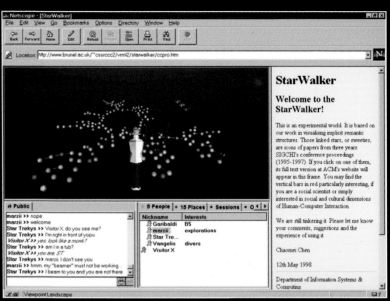

Semantic Constellations

Produced by Chaomei Chen from the Department of Information Systems and Computing at Brunel University, UK, Semantic Constellations are representations of over 150 conference papers from three years of online proceedings. They are formatted in a desktop VR environment, with the model generated in Virtual Reality Markup Language (VRML).

The structure has an arc-node configuration, with spheres standing for individual papers that are colour-coded by year. The arcs indicate semantic relationships between papers: the closer together two spheres are, the closer the semantic similarity between the papers. Pointing to a particular sphere causes the title of the paper to be shown in a pop-up window; clicking on a sphere displays a synopsis of the paper in a linked window.

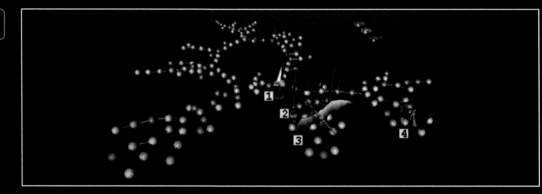

CASE STUDY

Loom2
Intuitively Visualizing Usenet Newsgroups

1

A landscape view depicts many subject areas and the relationships among them.

2

A medium-range view shows conversations within single groups, the topic of which is indicated typographically in grey.

3

A close-up view displays the individual's position in a conversation by bright-red type. General subject areas are shown in dim-red oblique type.

The Sociable Media Group in the MIT Media Lab, US, investigates issues concerning society and identity in the networked world. The emphasis is on design, building experimental interfaces and installations that explore new forms of social interaction.

Concept The main goal of Loom2 is to further our understanding of what are the most socio-culturally significant patterns in the domain of online conversations. Loom2 is a visualization tool for Usenet newsgroups, representing the pattern and layers of communication within a group. It is premised on the fact that innumerable patterns can be detected in the many statistical measures derived from an analysis of Usenet postings, yet only a few are sociologically important.

Structure As the name suggests, Loom2 uses the idea of a thread to chart the path of a person within the digital fabric or newsgroup. Thus, not only are the patterns of usage captured but also a historical context for the postings. The project's objective is to note any patterns in the key activities of a newsgroup, for example, the entry and exit of participants in conversation, the birth and death of subject threads, message tone and the path traversed by users as they form this social tapestry.

Context Loom2 generates many different mappings of the Usenet universe to provide a greater understanding of social patterns. Reinforcing the thread and weave metaphor, the visual system is structured in a 2-D grid that resembles the weave of a fabric. Circles fill the modules formed by the intersecting lines. Each circle represents a specific Usenet group and is labelled with its name. Groups of modules are delineated with light-grey lines, which define general subject areas, such as fashion, sports and sex.

Most data visualization systems are designed to display numerical data accurately and compactly, usually in the form of a graph. Its developers call Loom2 a 'social visualization', which conveys the meaning of the data as intuitively as possible. The visualizations are designed to be interfaces for the Usenet community and not for observers or marketeers.

ba.sports

alt.citadel.sports

fj.rec.sports

alt.flame.sports-suck

alt.sports.radio

clari.sports

alt.tv.sports

clari.web.sports.olympic

clari.web.sports.others

SPORTS

comp.sys.ibm.pc.misc

alt.pcnews

fr.comp.sys

alt.support.

misc.forsale.compu

PC

alt.penthouse.sex.women

alt.robots.sex

alt.sex.fetish.fashion
alt.fashion

alt.fashion.men
clari.living.fashion

FASHION

alt.religion.sexuality
alt.christnet.sex

alt.er.sex

alt.games.nettvshows.newsexpress

SEX

alt.books.crichton

fj.forsale.books

alt.marketplace.books.sf

aus.books

clari.living.books

3

2   1

4

An early Loom2 sketch explores the landscape view. This differs from image one in that it arranges circular modules around concentric circles.

5

A simplified use of modules and colour-coding, this is another early macro-level sketch.

6

Another early sketch uses type as the primary element.

7

A digitally refined sketch of image six without the structural elements – fabric weave, modules, subject area delineations – found in later versions.

4

5

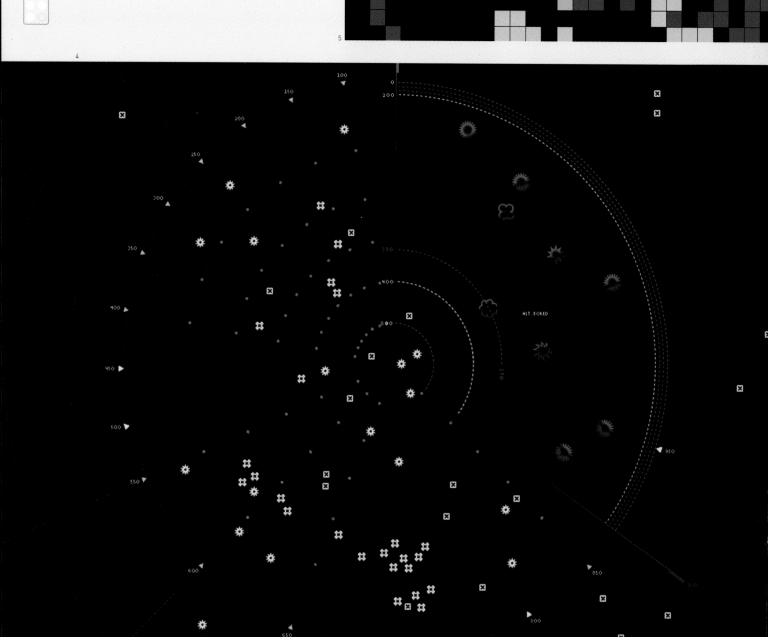

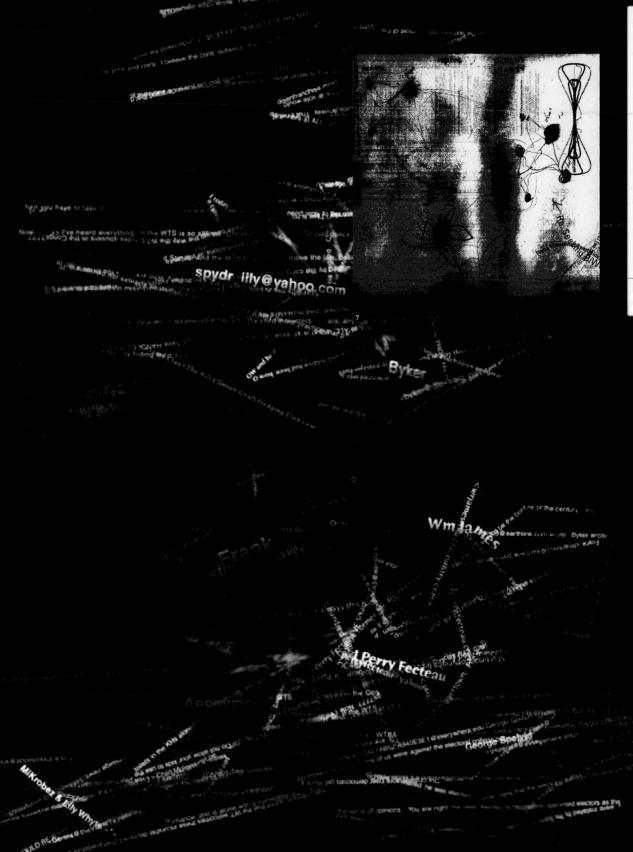

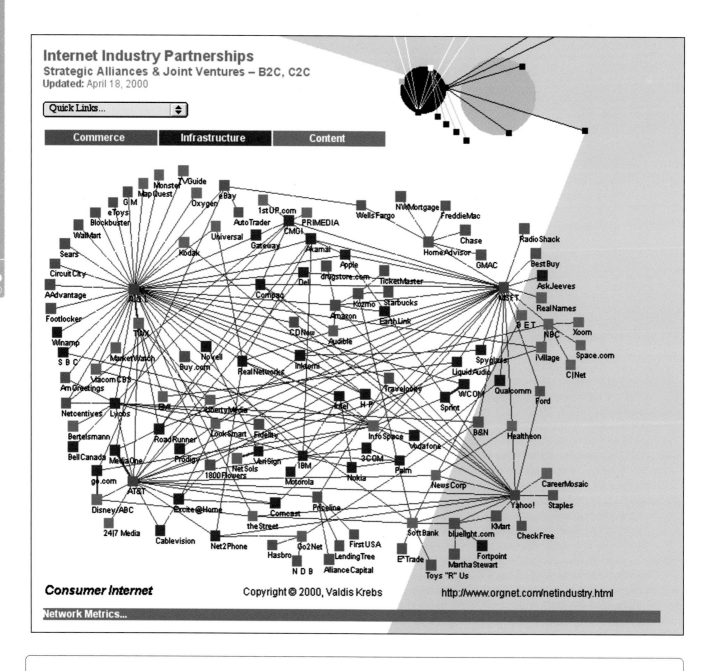

Internet Industry Partnerships
Strategic Alliances & Joint Ventures – B2C, C2C
Updated: April 18, 2000

Quick Links...

| Commerce | Infrastructure | Content |

Consumer Internet   Copyright © 2000, Valdis Krebs   http://www.orgnet.com/netindustry.html

Network Metrics...

Internet Industry Partnerships

Valdis Krebs assists international clients to build agile organizations by modelling and moulding knowledge networks and information flows.

The map demonstrates the forces that organizations put upon each other in complex, interconnected economic systems. Data is gathered from public sources and comprises information on business partnerships, such as strategic alliances, joint ventures, co-developments and investments.

Companies are judged on three metrics, derived from the overall pattern of industry partnerships:
1) Control: the degree to which a node controls the flow in the network and is a gatekeeper, or broker.
2) Access: how quickly a node can access the network's knowledge and information.
3) Reach: the extent to which nodes connect to other nodes via short paths.

The network metrics measure how well each node processes information flow and knowledge exchange in the industry network. A company with high scores on all three metrics will be well positioned to learn, adapt to and influence what is happening in the industry. These measurements highlight the advantage of 'being in the right place' in the network for exchanges of information, knowledge and resources.

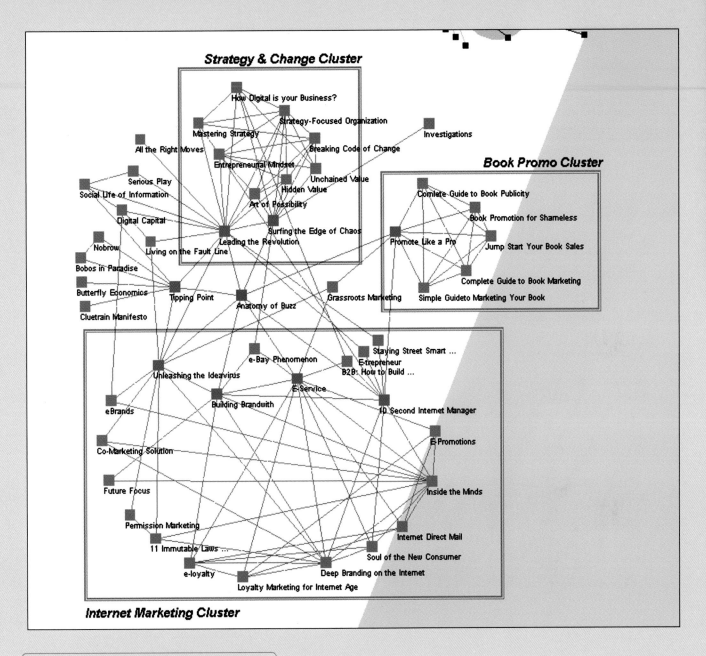

Strategy & Change Cluster

How Digital is your Business?
Strategy-Focused Organization
Investigations
Mastering Strategy
Breaking Code of Change
All the Right Moves
Entrepreneurial Mindset
Serious Play
Unchained Value
Social Life of Information
Hidden Value
Art of Possibility
Digital Capital
Surfing the Edge of Chaos
Nobrow
Living on the Fault Line
Leading the Revolution
Bobos in Paradise
Butterfly Economics
Tipping Point
Anatomy of Buzz
Grassroots Marketing
Cluetrain Manifesto

Book Promo Cluster

Comlete Guide to Book Publicity
Book Promotion for Shameless
Promote Like a Pro
Jump Start Your Book Sales
Complete Guide to Book Marketing
Simple Guideto Marketing Your Book

Internet Marketing Cluster

Staying Street Smart ...
e-Bay Phenomenon
E-trepreneur
B2B: How to Build ...
Unleashing the Ideavirus
E-Service
eBrands
Building Brandwith
10 Second Internet Manager
E-Promotions
Co-Marketing Solution
Inside the Minds
Future Focus
Permission Marketing
Internet Direct Mail
11 Immutable Laws ...
Soul of the New Consumer
e-loyalty
Deep Branding on the Internet
Loyalty Marketing for Internet Age

Communities of Interest Around the Book *Anatomy of Buzz*

A red line is drawn between two nodes (representing books) if they were bought together at a major web bookseller. The red node is *Anatomy of Buzz*, the green nodes are books tied directly (1 step) to the focus book, while the grey nodes are books that have an indirect relationship (2 steps) to the focus book. All these books are considered to fall within the network neighbourhood (i.e., the community of interest) of *Anatomy of Buzz*.

1
Organizational Network Mapping

Organization charts are a staple in human-resource departments. Used for control and planning, the chart displays who works where and who reports to whom. However, the rapid pace of today's business environment does not fit into static structures. A more appropriate model is Valdis Krebs's flexible, adaptable structure that organizes itself internally in response to external changes. In a knowledge-critical economy, the visualization of the complex connectivity that occurs in organizations is needed.

The organizational examples here represent several knowledge-management projects performed by Valdis Krebs. A key business process is shown, along with the knowledge exchanges that support it. The organization is seen from two perspectives. First, the company can be viewed in a hierarchical structure, an angle that reveals who is assigned where and who reports to whom. The company can also be depicted through emergent structures, which indicate where certain knowledge is clustered within the organization. Line thickness denotes the intensity of the relationship.

1 The chart is divided into four components:

1) Corporate HR Office, comprising Compensation and Benefits, HR Policy and HR Research

2) Strategic Business Unit 1 (SBU) HR Office

3) SBU 2 HR Office

4) SBU 3 HR Office

2 This formal organization structure clearly shows work flow, with most of the strong relationships appearing within the 'walls' of each particular company. Compensation and Benefits and HR Policy are firmly connected and seem to work as one unit. The SBUs' HR offices do not work with each other directly; most of their interaction is with the corporate HR office. This revelation alarmed the HR executive vice-president because all SBUs have similar missions, employee roles and numbers, and, therefore, should be talking to each other about any changes in their HR programme.

As a result, the most central node in each SBU was encouraged to arrange meetings with the other SBUs to share knowledge and experience and to develop good relationships.

3 Knowledge exchanges between companies are mapped here, showing how expertise is shared. A greater number of links between the SBUs are discovered, yet the corporate HR office still seems to hold most of the knowledge. R&D has fewer links within its department, but is now well connected to SBU 3, whose HR programme is left over from its former parent company. It would seem that

SBU 3 needs more interaction to adapt to this new system. It is interesting to compare the work-flow network with this one.

4–5 Communities reorganize themselves automatically around common problems, interests, customers and complex knowledge areas in an organization, and it is within these communities that an organization's core understanding is stored, shared and nurtured. Individual learning is improved by being a member of one or more communities of knowledge. The node's colour corresponds to a specific business unit (SBU 1

is yellow, SBU 2 green and SBU 3 grey), while the corporate HR office is represented by the icon. It is interesting that employees from SBU 1 are connected to each other in knowledge communities C and E but are not tied to community members from other organizations [4]. Fragmentation such as this is found in forming and dissolving communities. In this case, the communities were just forming in response to a change of environment and new direction from the corporate HR office.

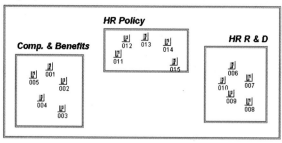

Corporate HR Office

HR Policy

Comp. & Benefits

HR R & D

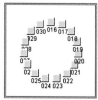

SBU 1 HR Office

SBU 3 HR Office

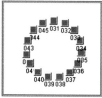

SBU 2 HR Office

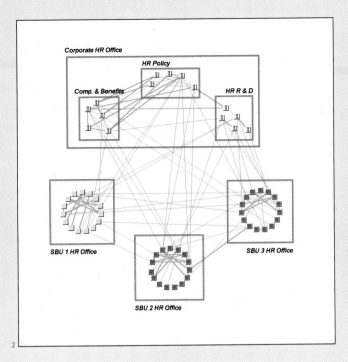

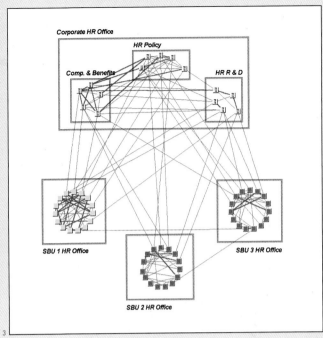

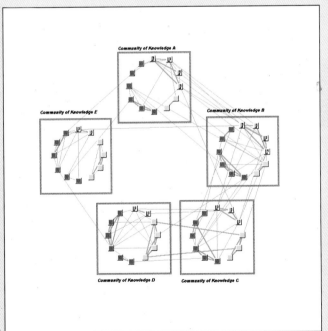

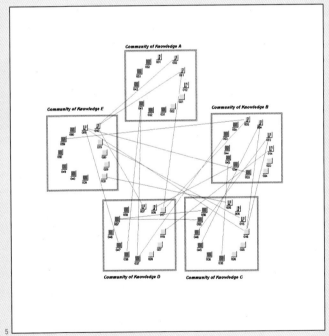

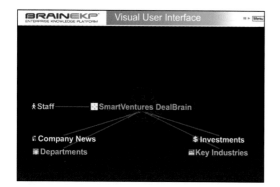

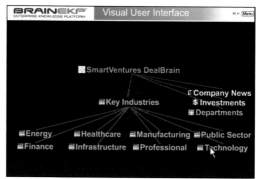

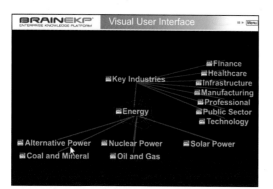

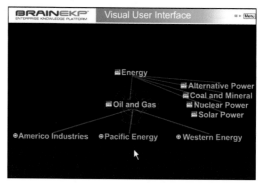

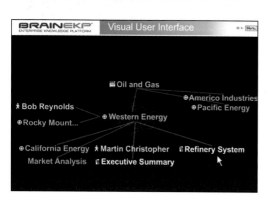

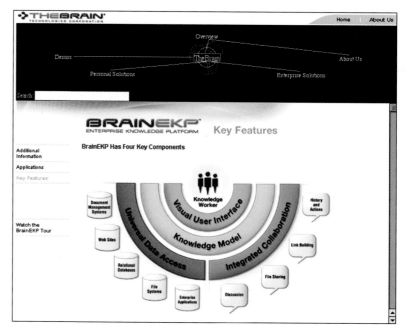

The Brain

Illustrating how information is related, offering a framework for collaboration and providing a visual context for documents and data, The Brain is an associative data organization system. Such information as files and webpages can be linked across applications in a network of logical associations.

Items in The Brain are called 'thoughts' and can be files, webpages or database records. The display is organized around a thought, surrounded by its related thoughts. Clicking on a thought brings it to the centre of the screen. Users quickly create structures that reflect the way they think about information. →

The Brain

Each item triggers related items, bringing relevant information as the user needs it. The simple actions of pointing and clicking let users visually browse the animated display. Information can be added and combined with existing data through a drag-and-drop process.

BrainEKP (Enterprise Knowledge Platform) comprises four key components. 'Universal Data Access' amalgamates information from many sources, from webpages to word-processing documents. 'Integrated Collaboration' enables communication in the place where information is created, stored and accessed. 'Knowledge Model' explains how the information is connected, accessed, processed and used. 'Visual User Interface' allows easy use and navigation of the system and shows how everything fits together.

In general business operations, processes or transactions when the 'time-to-resolution' is an important measure of performance, BrainEKP can provide a map of relevant companies, people, industry sectors and market analyses. The images presented here show BrainEKP used as the interface for the company website.

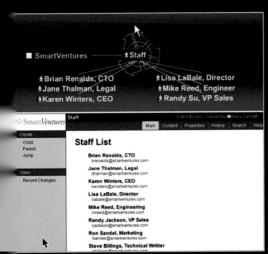

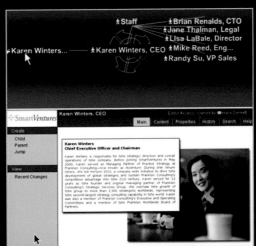

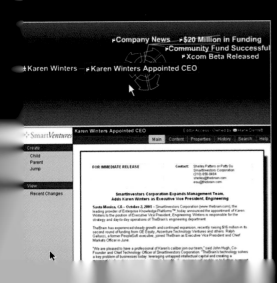

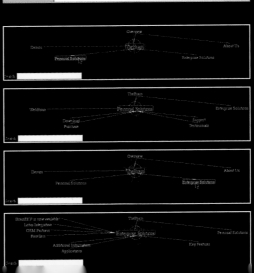

Visual Explanations
Communicating Critical Issues

XPLANE is internationally recognized for turning complex business issues into visual explanations that are easy to understand. It works with companies worldwide to communicate critical issues to customers, sales people, investors, employees or partners with clarity and meaning. AT&T, J.P. Morgan, PeopleSoft, Time Inc., Wired and Business 2.0 use XPLANATIONS (the visuals) to communicate simply and clearly to a global audience. XPLANATIONS are created in a variety of formats – static and interactive – for print or the web.

Project Title: Business 2.0

Concept *Business 2.0* is a magazine for business leaders in the new web economy. The magazine asked XPLANE to create a system for displaying high-tech information that gives internet entrepreneurs and business leaders 'need-to-know' news about the economy in the most efficient way.

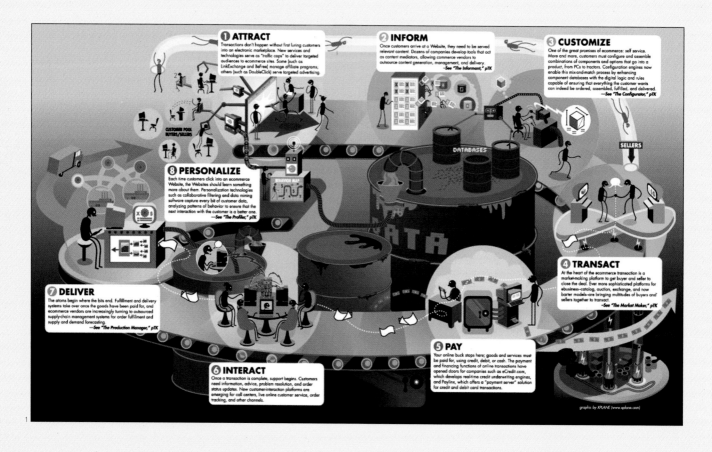

1 ATTRACT Transactions don't happen without first luring customers into an electronic marketplace. New services and technologies serve as "traffic cops" to deliver targeted audiences to ecommerce sites. Some (such as LinkExchange and BeFree) manage affiliate programs; others (such as DoubleClick) serve targeted advertising.

2 INFORM Once customers arrive at a Website, they need to be served relevant content. Dozens of companies develop tools that act as content mediators, allowing commerce vendors to outsource content generation, management, and delivery. —See "The Informant," pTK

3 CUSTOMIZE One of the great promises of ecommerce: self service. More and more, customers must configure and assemble combinations of components and options that go into a product, from PCs to tractors. Configuration engines now enable this mix-and-match process by enhancing component databases with the digital logic and rules capable of ensuring that everything the customer wants can indeed be ordered, assembled, fulfilled, and delivered. —See "The Configurator," pTK

8 PERSONALIZE Each time customers click into an ecommerce Website, the Websites should learn something more about them. Personalization technologies such as collaborative filtering and data mining software capture every bit of customer data, analyzing patterns of behavior to ensure that the next interaction with the customer is a better one. —See "The Profiler," pTK

4 TRANSACT At the heart of the ecommerce transaction is a market-making platform to get buyer and seller to close the deal. Ever more sophisticated platforms for ebusiness-catalog, auction, exchange, and now barter models-are bringing multitudes of buyers and sellers together to transact. —See "The Market Maker," pTK

7 DELIVER The atoms begin where the bits end. Fulfillment and delivery systems take over once the goods have been paid for, and ecommerce vendors are increasingly turning to outsourced supply-chain management systems for order fulfillment and supply and demand forecasting. —See "The Production Manager," pTK

5 PAY Your online buck stops here; goods and services must be paid for, using credit, debit, or cash. The payment and financing functions of online transactions have opened doors for companies such as eCredit.com, which develops realtime credit underwriting engines, and Paylinx, which offers a "payment server" solution for credit and debit card transactions.

6 INTERACT Once a transaction is complete, support begins. Customers need information, advice, problem resolution, and order status updates. New customer-interaction platforms are emerging for call centers, live online customer service, order tracking, and other channels.

graphic by XPLANE (www.xplane.com)

1

◆ **Structure** XPLANE worked with *B2* to create a modular system of highly functional XPLANATIONS with a memorable, high-energy feel. Presented here is 'Meet your Market Makers', which visualizes the relationship between two companies, Commerce One and Ariba. It illustrates how together they are establishing themselves as the builders and toll-collectors of the myriad of net market places.

✛ **Context** Drawing on the construction, plumbing and manufacturing trades, XPLANE created an iconographic map of the net marketplace. An intricate network of platforms contains fragmented and consolidated industries on the buyer-seller spectrum; underneath the platforms, Ariba is hard at work building the infrastructure and Commerce One is busy running the pipeline for the flow of goods, information and transactions.

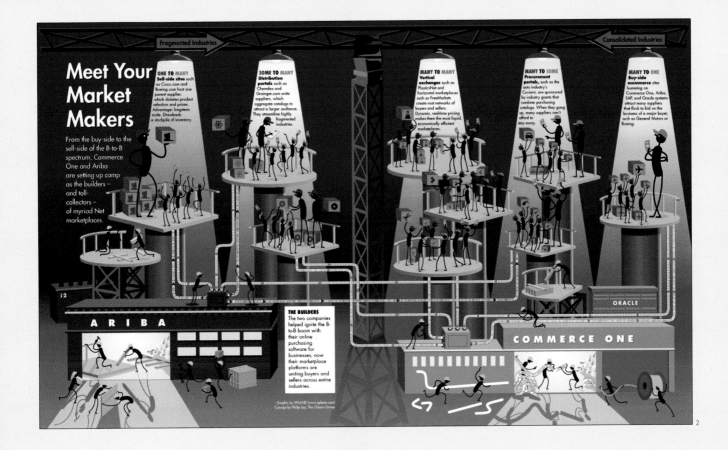

Within the illustration:

HotBot Web-search requests are sent through XML to several partners – top 10 sites, Web directories, and advertisers, among others. This month, HotBot will chuck HTML altogether to become the first major Web site to serve XML directly to compatible browsers.

INFOPORN

The Invisible WAN

Exposing XML's Backroom Connections

XML is knocking down walls all over town, but you're more likely to hear about it than see it. Originally hyped in the late '90s as HTML's successor on the Web, XML (extensible markup language) is instead spreading like kudzu behind the scenes, where its self-describing format lets programmers define and redefine tags to suit new purposes. Because XML is an open standard, companies can add or replace online partners without switching formats. That, plus heavy marketing from IBM, HP, Sun, and even Microsoft, gives XML star power with IT managers. As a result, balkanized companies can now remove longstanding technical and political barriers between servers and link their services to provide one-stop shopping to customers.

— Paul Boutin

Illustration by XPLANE (www.xplane.com)

Epicentric Autodesk provides its employees with an XML-fed intranet that's accessible by browser or phone. The portal carries customized news, stock prices, and other licensed content.

ShopTalk Marketplace Shoppers calling 1-800-SHOPTALK to order magazine subscriptions or Jiffy Lube coupons don't realize they're connecting to Tellme Networks. Tellme's voice-driven menu system browses ShopTalk services via … you guessed it.

Labels: Lycos, Direct Hit, Autodesk, HTML connection, search results, HotBot, CMPnet, ABC News, abc, Epicentric, Gofu.com, Internet Wire, iSyndicate, Reuters, Comtex, 121Jump, news and Features, ShopTalk, TELLME, HTML VILLAGE, Tellme servers, Microsoft, telephone connection, VoiceXML of ShopTalk menu selections

---

Concept *Wired* wanted to show how XML's (extensible mark-up language) data-linking abilities make it easy for clusters of related businesses to connect.

Structure XPLANE worked with *Wired* editors to create a four-page spread in the Infoporn section of the April 2001 issue (9.03, p. 81).

Context An axonometric cityscape portrays the pervasive and interconnected nature of XML within many industries: technology, publishing, transportation and retail.

Concept Explaining technologies in understandable chunks of information, be it for customers, clients or employees, is a new economy basic. Would you read a two-hundred-page paper of techno babble every time you were introduced to something new?

Structure + Context Flash and GIF have been frequently over-used. XPLANE needed to isolate the differences, advantages and pitfalls of the two graphic formats for the web. To do this, XPLANE came up with a useful Flash movie that was amusing, concise and informative.

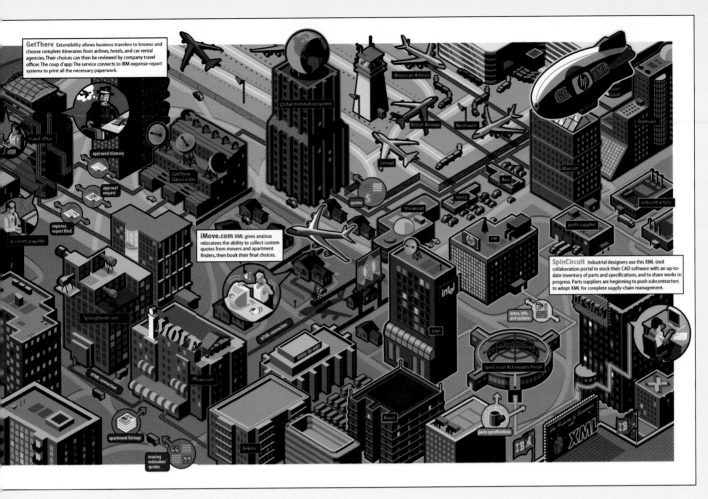

GetThere Extensibility allows business travelers to browse and choose complete itineraries from airlines, hotels, and car rental agencies. Their choices can then be reviewed by company travel officer. The coup d'app: The service connects to IBM expense-report systems to print all the necessary paperwork.

iMove.com XML gives anxious relocatees the ability to collect custom quotes from movers and apartment finders, then book their final choices.

SpinCircuit Industrial designers use this XML-ized collaboration portal to stock their CAD software with an up-to-date inventory of parts and specifications, and to share works in progress. Parts suppliers are beginning to push subcontractors to adopt XML for complete supply-chain management.

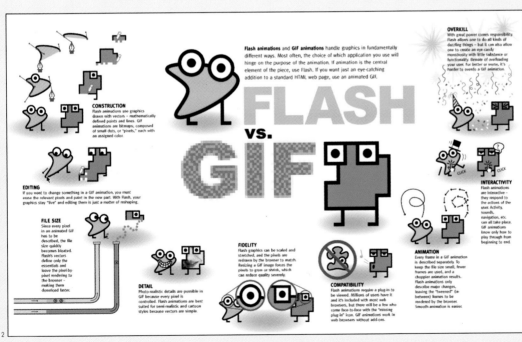

Flash animations and **GIF animations** handle graphics in fundamentally different ways. Most often, the choice of which application you use will hinge on the purpose of the animation. If animation is the central element of the piece, use Flash. If you want just an eye-catching addition to a standard HTML web page, use an animated GIF.

FLASH vs. GIF

CONSTRUCTION
Flash animations use graphics drawn with vectors – mathematically defined points and lines. GIF animations are bitmaps, composed of small dots, or "pixels," each with an assigned color.

EDITING
If you want to change something in a GIF animation, you must erase the relevant pixels and paint in the new part. With Flash, your graphics stay "live" and editing them is just a matter of reshaping.

FILE SIZE
Since every pixel in an animated GIF has to be described, the file size quickly becomes bloated. Flash's vectors define only the essentials and leave the pixel-by-pixel rendering to the browser – making them download faster.

DETAIL
Photo-realistic details are possible in GIF because every pixel is controlled. Flash animations are best suited for semi-realistic and cartoon styles because vectors are simple.

FIDELITY
Flash graphics can be scaled and stretched, and the pixels are redrawn by the browser to match. Resizing a GIF image forces the pixels to grow or shrink, which can reduce quality severely.

COMPATIBILITY
Flash animations require a plug-in to be viewed. Millions of users have it and it's included with most web browsers, but there will be a few who come face-to-face with the "missing plug-in" icon. GIF animations work in web browsers without add-ons.

ANIMATION
Every frame in a GIF animation is described separately. To keep the file size small, fewer frames are used, and a choppier animation results. Flash animations only describe major changes, leaving the "tweened" (in-between) frames to be rendered by the browser. Smooth animation is easier.

OVERKILL
With great power comes responsibility. Flash allows one to do all kinds of dazzling things – but it can also allow one to create an eye-candy monstrosity with little substance or functionality. Beware of overloading your user. For better or worse, it's harder to overdo a GIF animation.

INTERACTIVITY
Flash animations are interactive – they respond to the user. Activity, sounds, navigation, etc. can all take place. GIF animations know only how to play through from beginning to end.

2

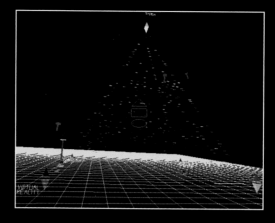

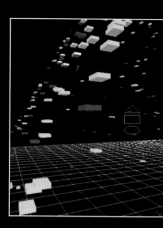

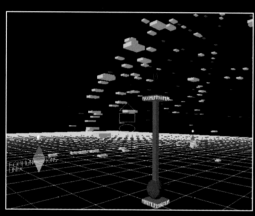

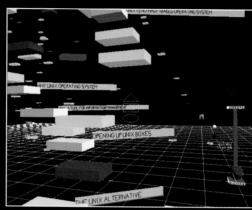

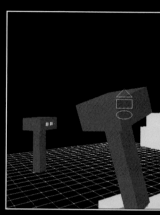

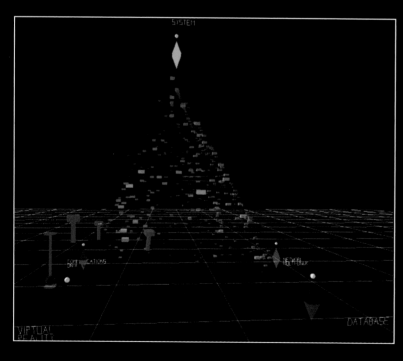

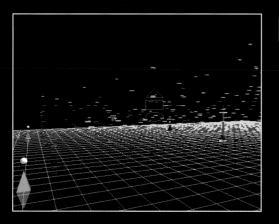

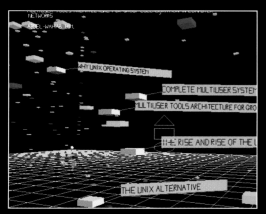

Populated Information Terrain

Developed by Dave Snowdon, Steve Benford and colleagues at the University of Nottingham, UK, PIT is an advanced VR (virtual reality) system that allows multiple participants to interact with information and collaborate with each other in a digital environment. PIT derives its name from its key aim; the visualizations are intended to be multi-user applications in which users virtually inhabit the database environment and are visible to one another. There are many techniques for generating the visualizations, but the method used in VR-VIBE, a bibliographic database at the University of Nottingham, is exhibited here.

Users specify key words, represented by octahedrons, that they wish to be used in the bibliographical visualization and place them in the 3-D space. A 3-D scrollbar allows less relevant documents to be filtered out by changing the value of the relevance threshold. Relevance is determined by the number of key-word matches within a document.

A document equally spaced between two key words is equally relevant to both, while a document close to a single key word is particular to that word alone. The more relevant the document, the brighter its colour. This distinction is necessary to distinguish between a document that

is only remotely relevant to a key word, but is next to a document that is highly relevant to two key words and has, therefore, been placed between (but some distance from) the two words.

The VR-VIBE system brings computer data and the human closer through its statistical methods, which analyze collections of data (usually documents) and group objects together according to semantic relationships, i.e., relationships according to meaning and logic as opposed to the way humans think and organize information.

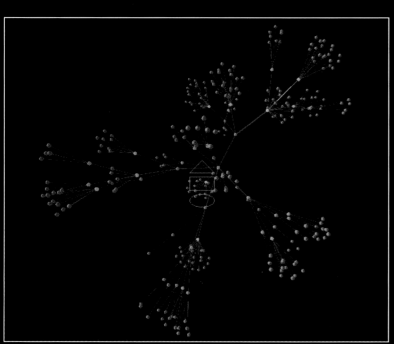

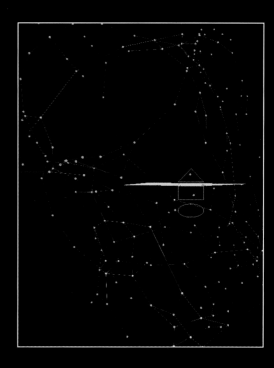

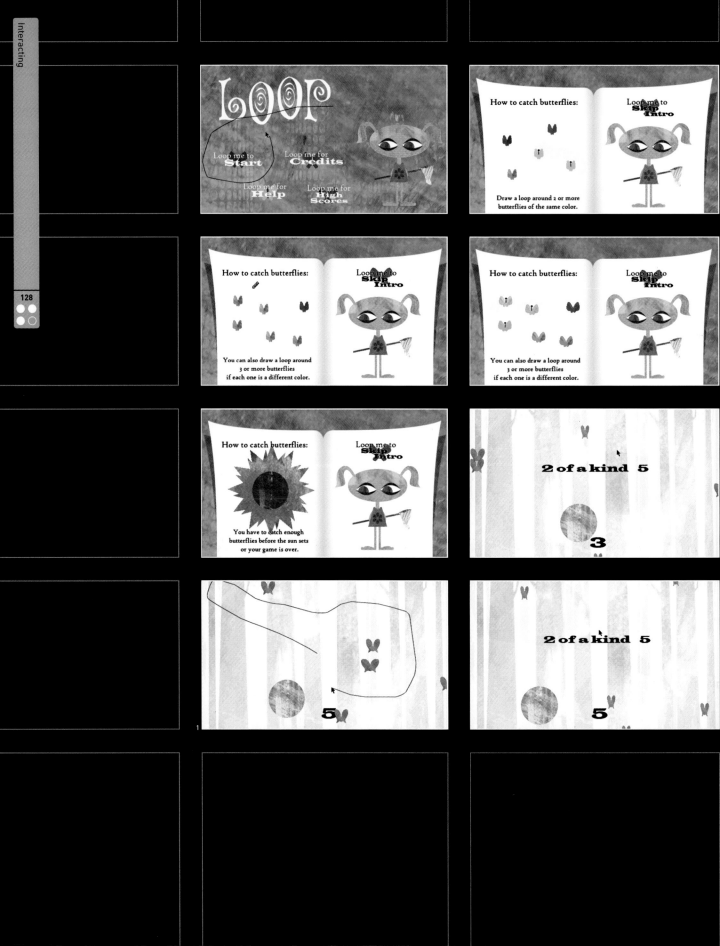

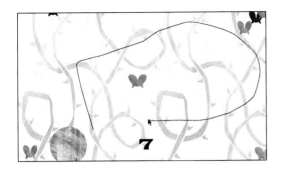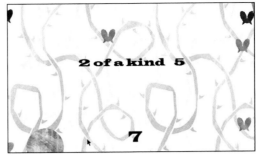

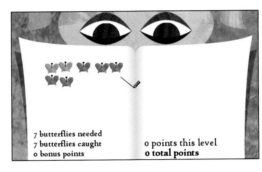

sanctioned mischief

emergent play

procedural
transformation

mediated uncertainty

space of possibility

artificial conflict

sanctioned mischief

meaningful choice

2

1–3
GameLab

Founded by Eric Zimmerman and Peter Lee, GameLab is a startup game-development company that attempts to break ground by finding new audiences, inventing original forms of gameplay and exploring narrative content and audiovisual styles not normally found in mainstream 'Hollywood-style' games. They come up with ideas and then search for a publisher who is willing to fund the creation process, manufacture, marketing and distribution of the product.

Game design requires a different approach to website design. A website delivers a piece of information to the user; thus, planning proceeds backward from the end user's viewpoint to establish the method of interaction and build the interface. In game design, the interaction is the experience, which contains inherent unpredictability. Games are designed around simple rules, creating engaging play that tests hand-eye dexterity. GameLab believes that gameplay is more important than the graphic assimilation of reality, an approach that is purposefully on the fringe in contrast to the multimillion-dollar, super-realism games released by the major companies.

GameLab's philosophy is captured in its visual identity [3], a system of diagrams that illustrates the kinds of interactivity found in gameplay: emergent play, mediated uncertainty, artificial conflict, meaningful choice, sanctioned mischief and procedural transformation.

LOOP [1–2], a game available on Shockwave.com, is set in the imagination of a little girl named Ada, who is reading a book. In her dreams she catches butterflies, with the help of the game players. It is designed to be played on multiplayer computer desktops. The game is played without pushing any keys or clicking on the mouse; only the rolling action of the mouse is required, the movement of which is represented by a pencil icon on the screen.

The play space is a dreamy collage of flowers, leaves, butterflies, spiders, bees and the sun, inspired by children's book illustrator Eric Carle who created *The Very Hungry Caterpillar*. The player draws loops, by rolling the mouse, around butterflies of the same colour. The number of butterflies that need to be caught to complete the game successfully is presented on each page of the book. An audio track heightens the overall experience.

3

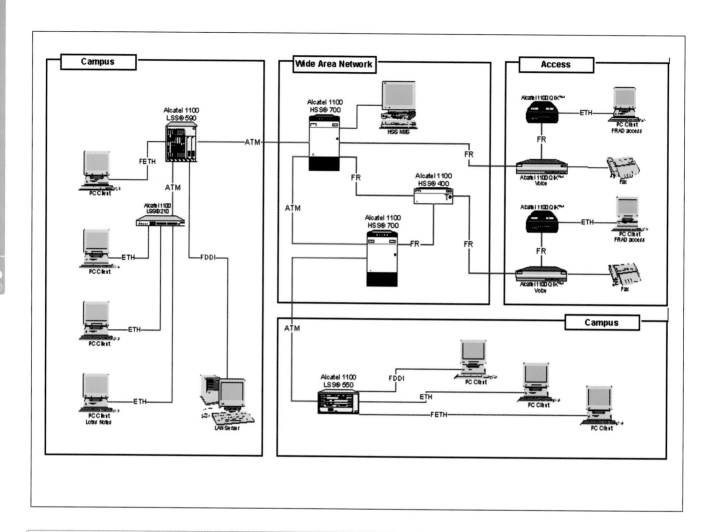

SmartDraw

Allowing people to 'draw anything easily', SmartDraw is diagramming software. It creates a variety of diagrams, such as flow charts, decision trees, organizational charts, network diagrams, floor plans, mechanical or chemical diagrams, maps and posters. An extensive selection of symbols and templates give users of all abilities the potential to visualize their needs.

A number of features make the experience efficient and easily customized. SmartDraw Explorer enables the user to browse for symbols or search by name or key word. A built-in 'Hints' guide assists with the first drawing and the buttons on the toolbar are automatically labelled. Libraries contain the symbols and templates, or users can develop a personal list of symbols.

SmartDraw accommodates up to sixteen open windows at any one time. Shapes can be decomposed into their component lines and curves for individual manipulation, or users can begin from scratch. Editing an existing symbol allows users to define where text will be positioned and how it will resize when stretched or scaled. The lines that join the shapes remain connected even when moved or resized.

The final diagram is completely dependent on the subject matter and complexity of information. Diagrams can be printed out for publishing purposes and presentations, or exported as HTML files with working hyperlinks to be uploaded on the web. All versions of SmartDraw act as an OLE server, allowing the diagrams to be embedded into such programs as Microsoft Word, Excel and PowerPoint. Drawings can contain thousands of shapes and lines. Shown here are diagrams about computer networks.

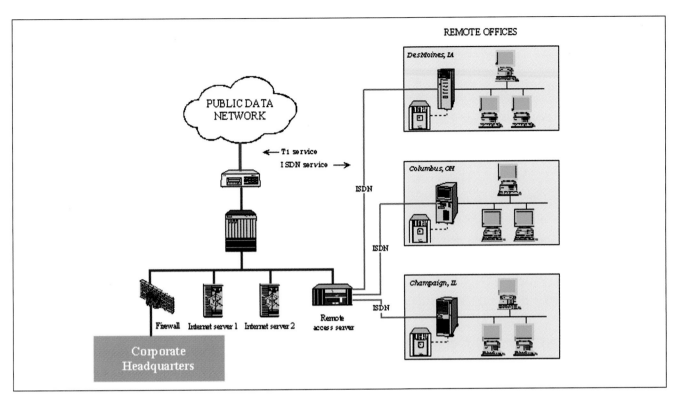

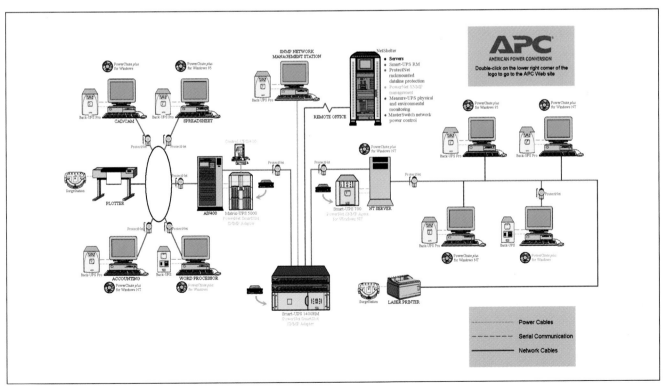

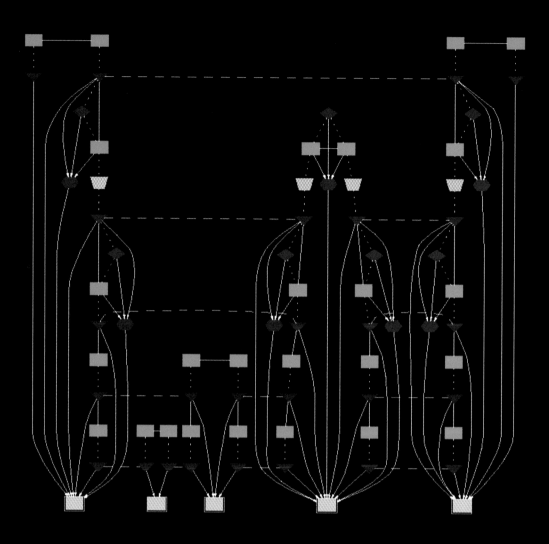

1

GraphViz

To visualize the structural information of graphs and networks, Graphviz creates representations geometrically. Generating graphs assists such key technologies as database design, software engineering and network design. To meet the demand for a tool that would display and manipulate graphs, Graphviz came up with a basic graph that fits a broad range of algorithms and programs. Researchers produced a tool kit of libraries and programs that create, filter, display and interact with graphs. Formulated for Unix or Windows, Graphviz's system comprises several tools: 'Dot' forms hierarchical layouts of directed graphs; 'Neato' makes 'spring model' layouts of undirected graphs; 'Dotty' is an interface written in LEFTY (a programmable graphics editor that displays graphs in a way that users can manipulate them); 'TCLdot' is an interface written in TCL; and 'Libgraph' is the library for graph tools.

'Dotty' is the most important tool for the average user, providing menu-driven commands for loading or creating graphs, performing edits and saving changes. It can easily be customized by modifying the LEFTY program and by redefining the interface functions.

Three families of graph layout algorithms have been successful: hierarchical layouts of trees and DAGS (directed acyclic graphs), virtual-physical ('spring model') layouts of undirected graphs and orthogonal grid layouts of planarized graphs. Graphviz makes the first two using 'Dot' and 'Neato', which read graphs, compute layouts and write the graphs either for layouts in graphic language (Postscript, GIF) or as attributed graphs whose objects have associated layout coordinates.

Comprehensive diagrams of reasonably sized graphs and scalable large graphs are produced by Graphviz's algorithms. Graphviz also creates convenient graph-drawing systems and web services by defining useful interfaces and features to support applications.

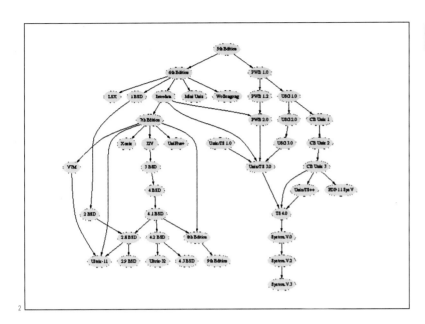

GraphViz

1 The graph represents the architecture of an Open System's Interconnection (OSI) protocol stack.
2 The earliest example of GraphViz, the graph was originally hand-drawn in 1984. It illustrates the evolution of the UNIX operating system.
3 Generated automatically, the image shows the relationship between a graphic interface and a standard debugger.
4 A diagram of a sort program's dynamic profile.
5 An example of the ability of 'Dot' to draw nodes and edges in clusters or in separate rectangular layouts.

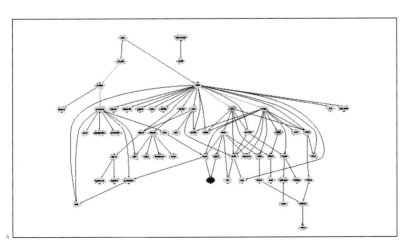

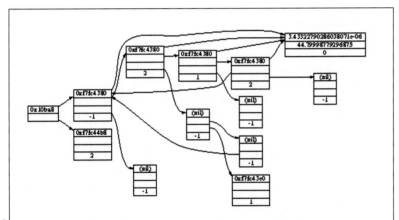

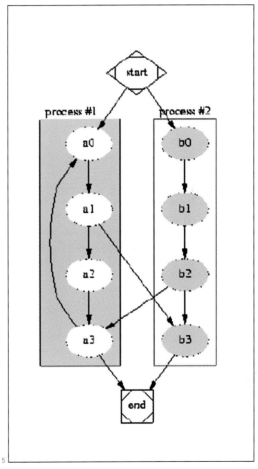

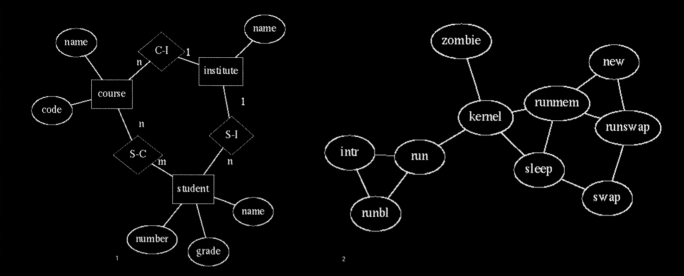

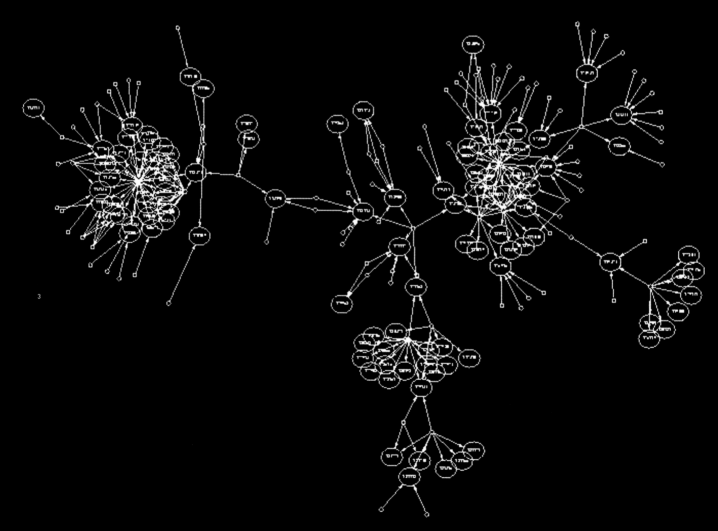

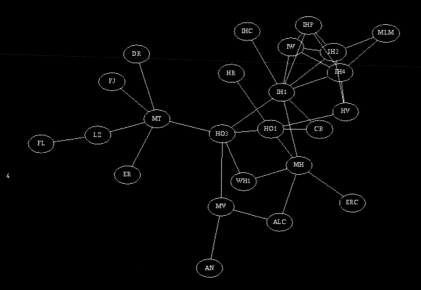

1–6
GraphViz

1–2 Layouts made with 'Neato' tend to make sure that the edges are about the same length (unless a manual adjustment is made).

3 Testing large programs is difficult and expensive. The purpose of this graph is to find which sets of modifications can be made without having a knock-on effect in other areas of the program.

4 A graph of an intranet. Notice how a connected subgraph has been created between the nodes IHP, IW, IH1, IH2 and IH4.

5 Taken from Forrester's book *World Dynamics*, the graph has been adapted by GraphViz to add 'same rank' constraints to find a heuristic solution to edge crossing.

6 This is a left-to-right drawing of a finite automaton in a landscape format.

135

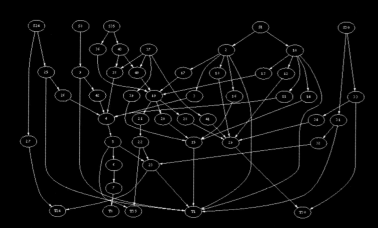

5

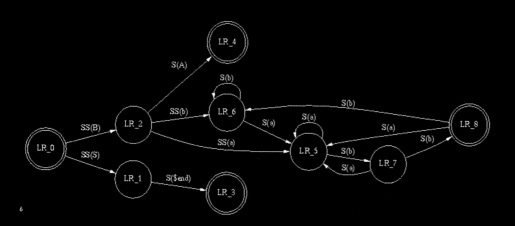

6

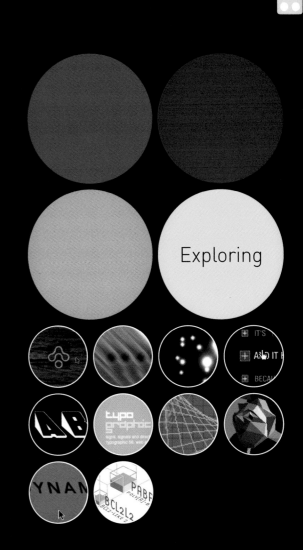

Exploring

Exploring

Pushing today's technology to its limits to find new ways of navigating a website or working with the computer.

The creation and distribution of media is undergoing radical changes. A communication environment has emerged in which all media – text, sound and dynamic and static images – have converged into one form: the digital. At the same time, media presentation is becoming increasingly divergent and we are able to access media from a wide variety of devices. This does not mean print is dead; the future of publishing – creating and distributing media – is no longer product-specific, but media neutral. The lifeblood of this is computer source code.

Graphic designers are beginning to embrace computation as the way of improving the quality and richness of media communication and expression. Artists and designers have always welcomed the latest technology to realize what had been unimaginable outcomes, for example,

the printing press, the camera, the desktop computer and now PDAs.

The synthesis of art and technology with the goal of communication, graphic design visually transmits thoughts, messages or information to an audience. The primary method of communication remains text. The twenty-six letters of the Western alphabet are the oldest human-made objects in use today and are not about to disappear with digital technology still in its infancy. However, new systems of recording, editing, transferring and receiving textual information have always influenced fresh paradigms of visual aesthetics, from typeface design to typographic composition and reproduction.

The challenge for many website and interface designers today is to identify and to take advantage of the differences between design

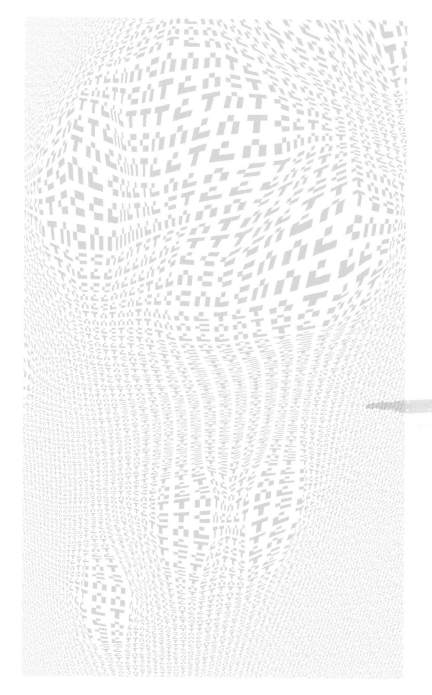

for print and design for screen. Countless books, journals, articles, conferences and competitions have heralded the successes (and failures) of this new area of design. Discussions about the differences between print and digital among professionals, academics and students are endless but valuable. The underlying feeling is that we are venturing into new territory, which everyone wants to master and exploit.

Contained on the following pages are cases that demonstrate a spirit of exploration into the unknown and untried by adventurers skilled in computer coding and visual design. Often, these experiments serve creative ends; other times, they provide key components for evolving a new method of website navigation or computer interaction. 'Exploring' has no specific directive, but asks the simple question 'what if?'. What if letters could move in space? What if we synthesize the physical city with the digital city? What if we could paint with pixels? What if the internet could be as tactile as the printed page?

Chromosome 22
The DNA 'alphabet' consists of four letters – G, A, C, T – which stand for DNA's chemical components Guanosine, Adenosine, Cytosine and Thymidine.

The letters can form endless numbers of sequences. Here, Ben Fry has created an interactive program that allows users to explore the 48-million-letter sequence for Chromosome 22. A three-pixel font is used at a resolution of 200 pixels per inch. This image is one quarter of the entire chromosome. The user can push and pull the space to look at specific features.

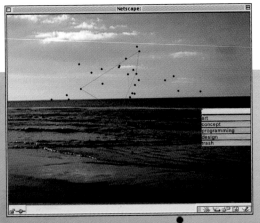

video
concept

Sinnzeug

An unusual and dynamic search engine, Sinnzeug uncovers links to intelligent websites that the creators – Stephan Huber, Ralph Ammer, Birte Steffan – have concluded are worthy of spending time on. All the websites are special, whether they exhibit beautiful programming ideas, are up-to-date online magazines or feature experimental art. Sinnzeug is a non-commercial project that requires the latest shockwave plug-in – many of the sites in the search engine allow extensive interaction using this application.

Black dots slowly appear against a serene beachscape. Each dot represents a website. When the user has compiled the catchword index the dots will migrate toward the word with which they feel they have the most in common. Lines are drawn between visited sites so users can trace back to the websites they might have enjoyed during a prior use of Sinnzeug.

An icon and name of a site will temporarily appear when the mouse rolls over a dot and doubleclicking on the dot takes the user to the site. By doubleclicking anywhere in the window users can enter a key word or choose one from a pop-up menu. An individual search for websites is started by placing an index of catchwords (such as 'art', 'programming', 'concept') in the window. A catchword can be eliminated by dragging it out of the window.

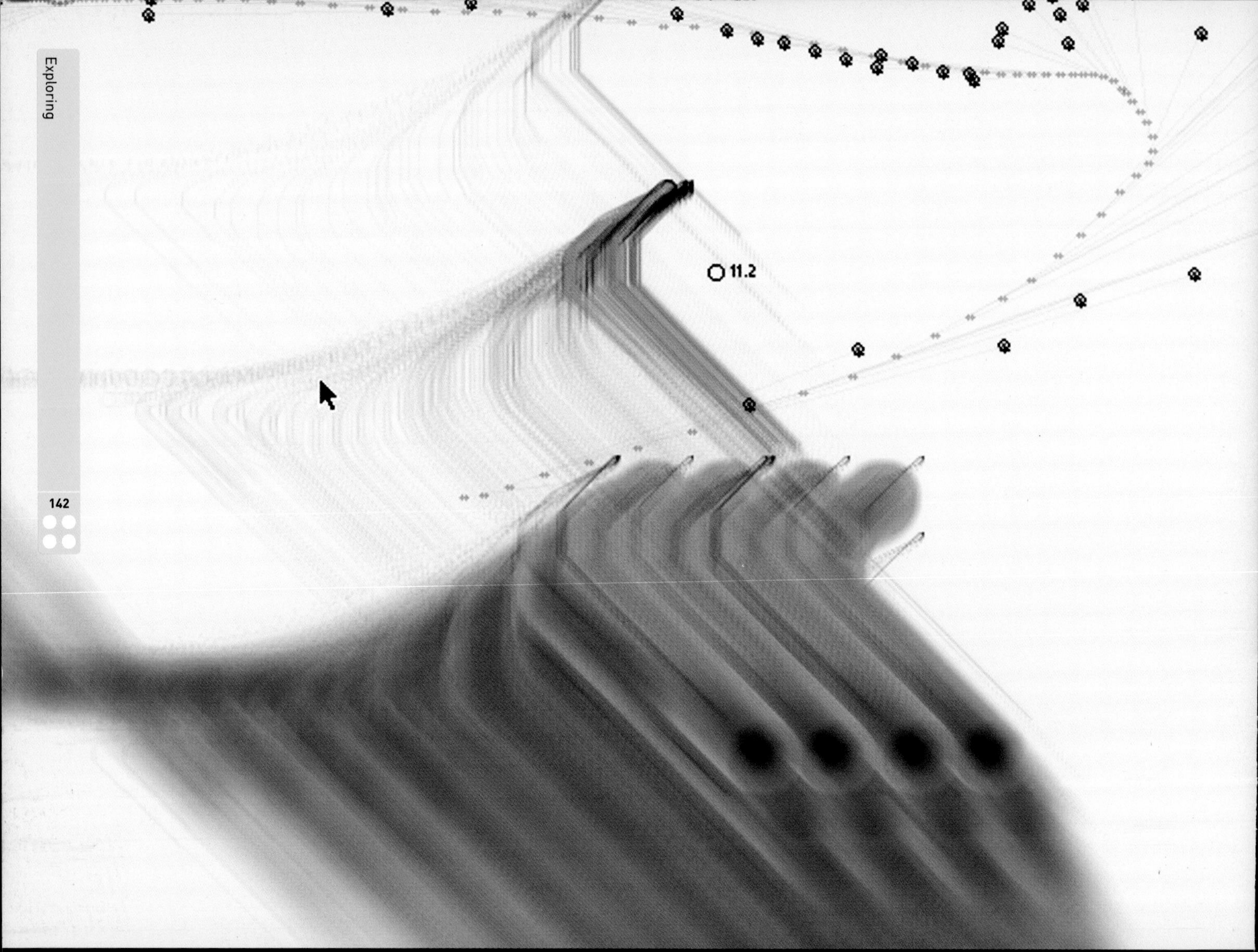

11.2

Turux

Viennese design group Dextro is interested in infusing digital interactive media with a level of sensuality never perceived through the visually impotent CRT or LCD monitor screen. The group makes interactive animations or drawings because it believes that showing finished, static pictures is like claiming a territory. The designers' intention is to motivate people to create something by themselves. With this in mind, Dextro has developed a complex scripting program with Macromedia Director that incorporates human feelings, such as attraction and repulsion. The group's aim is to find new visual behaviour in the smallest visual element produced by the computer: the pixel. These dots of light release themselves into unpredictable yet elegant performances beneath the surface of the screen. The dot animations possess a certain tactility, a difficult feat when the viewer is separated from the action by a smooth, cold window. A clue to the inspiration behind these dynamic visualizations of binary data is a web link tagged with the question, 'is ghb a toxic, addictive, severe – drowsiness – hallucinations – confusion – convulsions – combative – and – self – injurious – behaviour – respiratory – arrest – seizures – coma – and – finally – death – inducing soon – to – become – illegal grievous – bodily – harm new designer date – rape drug?'

Rhizome
An Experimental Online Environment for New Media Art

Rhizome is an online community space for people who are interested in new media art – any type of contemporary art that uses digital technology. The site focuses on presenting artwork by new media artists, critics and curators, fostering critical dialogue between these parties and preserving media art for the future.

The community space not only provides an important context for this artform, it also helps to create it. The alt.interface (short for 'alternate interface') section of the website showcases new visual interfaces that artists have designed to help visitors browse the website.

Project Title: Every Image [1–4]

 Concept Every Image is a software program that travels across the internet

to collect images and text for the Rhizome.org online database. The program presents this information in the form of a screen saver, which is a software application that runs to protect the CRT screen of the monitor when the computer is shut down.

 Structure + Navigation
Pictures are retrieved from the Rhizome server at random, transferred over the internet and displayed, like a slide show, on the computer screen. Each illustration is taken from the history of internet art – documentation of other art projects, exhibition announcements, image fragments – with the oldest images dating to 1996. With each passing day the pool of images grows and mutates.

Context Every Image consists of a set of Perl scripts running on a Linux server. It relies on the ImageMagick Perl software for all real-time graphics manipulation and is internet-based in content as well as form. Each new picture is digitally altered by Every Image to affect an overall mood. First the image is made slightly blue in colour and a touch darker, then it is cropped to a specific ratio and enlarged to accentuate each pixel. In effect an internet 'readymade', the screen savers combine images from many different sources and time periods. Install Every Image on your computer, wait a moment and then a beautiful narrative spanning the last five years of net art will unfold before you.

1 Resistance and Maps Ricardo Dominguez Ours is not the house of pain and misery. That is how he who robs and deceives us has painted us. Ours is not the land of death and anguish. Ours is not the treason nor does our way have room for the forgetting. Ours are not the empty ground and the hollow sky. Ours is the house of light and joy. That is how we created it, that is how we struggle

(Soda) wrote: The Bureau's strategy of being at all points in the cycle, or system, in the production of works (making the work, tech stuff, conceptual, design and packaging) is an interesting one for other artists to consider. I'd say the Bureau's

artists Jenny Ulthoff/Alexander Vaindorf and Kiki Sekor at Apex Art as part of the "222"--two curators, two artists, two projects, series. It seems that there have been a lot of well-intended but ultimately disappointing attempts made to bring

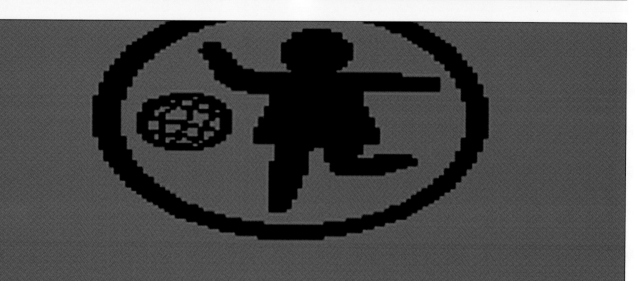

Boyadjiev By Geert Lovink Hybrid Workspace, Documenta X, Kassel June 20, 1997 Luchezar Boyadjiev (Sofia, 1957) is working currently as an artist. His background is studies in art history and theory, pursued both in Bulgaria and the United

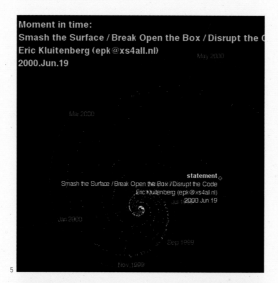

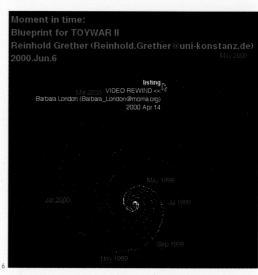

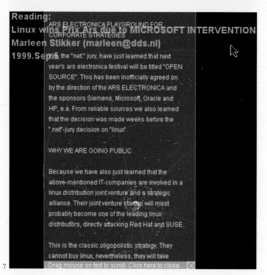

Project Title: Spiral [**5–7**]

Concept Spiral is a new interface artwork for viewing and browsing Rhizome.org's library of over 1,700 indexed and edited texts, all of which were submitted by members of the Rhizome community.

Structure + Context Each text is represented by a star in the spiral-shaped timeline and its location is determined by the date it was added to the library. The oldest texts appear at the bottom of the spiral, while the newest texts are at the top. The texts are indexed by category, to allow for easy searching.

Navigation The user moves the mouse over a star to view information about its corresponding text; to read the text, the user clicks on the star. The right-hand-side scrollbar takes the visitor forward or backward in time.

Project Title: StarryNight [**8–11**]

Concept To quote *The Independent on Sunday* (London, 18 July 1999), 'StarryNight is the way into an archive of messages held by Rhizome. At a time when the world is looking at the Net and seeing a welter of ballooning stock options, the idea of visualising part of it as a thousand points of light harks back to its early dreams, in which it would take us to a high dimension, and everybody in it would be a star.'

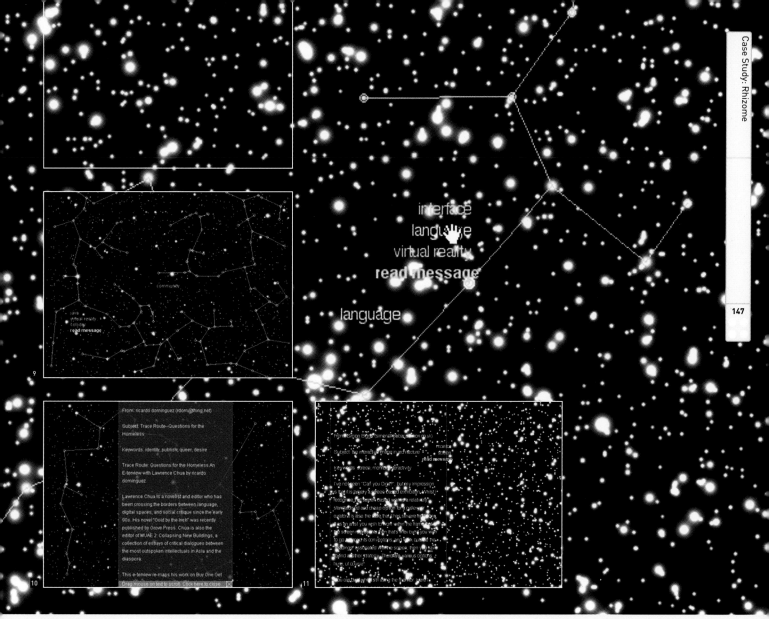

Structure StarryNight depends on two pieces of original software: a set of Perl scripts that sorts texts by key word and records their individual hits and a Java applet that filters this information and draws the stars and constellations.

Context When a new text is read for the first time on the Rhizome website, it appears on StarryNight as a dim star. Each star gets brighter the more often it is visited. Over time the page comes to resemble a starry night sky. The brightness of the stars is updated daily, with new stars added weekly.

Navigation Dragging the mouse over one of the stars brings up a pop-up list of key words that the text shares with other texts. By selecting a word from the list, a constellation is drawn that links all the stars that share the key word.

1

MONO*CRAFTS 3.0 (2)

2000.12.20 23:50:30
01: TREE-DESCRIPTION 01
SURFACE | | | | INFO ► 2001.07.20 : FG2001 CONFERENCE: KOREA 2001.07.29-31

2

2000.12.20 23:50:30
01: TREE-DESCRIPTION 01
SURFACE | | | |

(3)

MONO*CRAFTS 3.0 (2)

HAS JUST STARTED (1)

SURFACE.YUGOP.COM (3)

IT'S (1)

AND IT HAS (1)

BECAUSE IT'S (1)

WILL SOON RELEASE (1)

WILL SOON RELEASE

2000.12.20 23:50:30
01: TREE-DESCRIPTION 01
SURFACE | | | | INFO ► 2001.05.01 : SHIFT COVER AND INTERVIEW

2000.12.20 23:50:30
01: TREE-DESCRIPTION 01
SURFACE | | | |

4

5

1–6
MONO*crafts

Yugo Nakamura (Japan) runs
MONO*crafts, his personal
net-based laboratory, where
he explores every possible
form of visual expression on
the web. One of his primary
interests is the construction
of innovative human–
computer interfaces.

Nakamura's 'Tree
Description 01' is a visual
map (in a simple tree layout)
of his study of surface and
structure. The tree
incorporates fluid motion
and changes with user
interaction. Nakamura
describes surface.yugop.com

as 'ephemeral', 'improvised'
and 'inconsistent'.
Conversely, he uses the
words 'steady', 'elaborated'
and 'tightly organized' to
refer to structure.yugop.com.

By separating the meaning
of surface and structure
into independent concepts,
Nakamura almost
establishes them as being in
opposition to one another.
The user first sees a black
space in which the name of
the studio floats with a slight
back-and-forth motion [1].
When the small box
containing the plus symbol

(to the left of the studio
name) is clicked on, the plus
turns into a minus symbol
and two links emerge [2].
Each link has a short,
provocative phrase, such
as 'has just started', or 'will
soon release', which rouses
the user's curiosity. The
entire tree structure shifts
more and more dramatically
with each node that is
clicked on. So, the more
nodes the user clicks, the
more links emerge and the
larger the structure grows
[3–6], eventually outgrowing
the user's window.

☐ MONO*CRAFTS 3.0 (2)

⊞ HAS JUST STARTED (1)

⊞ WILL SOON RELEASE (1)

☐ MONO*CRAFTS 3.0 (2)

☐ HAS JUST STARTED (1)

⊞ SURFACE.YUG...M (3)

⊞ WILL SOON RELEASE (1)

2000.12.20 23:50:30 ●
01: TREE-DESCRIPTION 01

05.14 IdN FRESHCONFERENCE SYDNEY 2001.09.28-29

⊞ IT'S (1)

⊞ AND IT HAS (1)

☐ BECAUSE IT'S (1)

⊞ JUST (1)

☐ SURFACE.YUGOP.COM (3)

☐ IT'S (1)

☐ SO (3)

▢ EPHEMERAL, (0)

▢ IMPROVISED, (0)

▢ INCONSISTENT. (0)

⊞ AND IT HAS (1)

2000.12.20 23:50:30 ●
01: TREE-DESCRIPTION 01

05.14 IdN FRESHCONFERENCE SYDNEY 2001.09.28-29

identity

e-Types
information
typography
work
revolution
tools

WORK
corporate
identity
publications
moving media

IDENTITY
eurowoman
nt-video
prey4.com
steelvision
torvehallen
underværket
mostrup
ds dental
D.L. Clement

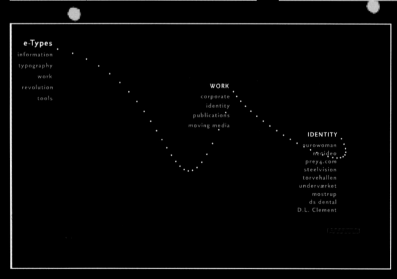

e-Types

Danish design firm and type foundry e-Types delivers surprising eloquence and structure through its interface. When users enter the site, their eyes are drawn across a plain black field to a pulsating white 'e' that turns into the firm's logotype and proceeds to form a menu. Users are immediately invited to playfully compose and scale this information, and their work takes the form of 3-D arching dotted lines and pulsating rhythms against a barren black landscape.

Users receive instructions to drag the logotype and menu to various points in the window or to doubleclick to scale the information. A box, called Navigator, appears in the lower-right corner with such selections as 'in', 'out', 'centre' and 'reset'. Within Navigator, a translucent red box portrays the physical results of the text options. It also acts as a viewfinder within a larger field of play, indicating the position of the main menu and submenus with a pulsing red dot. Each action changes the user's orientation to the type. The website is a fluid montage, with animated sequences of the firm's work interwoven with the site's organic navigation.

1–4
Typographic 56

This design group focuses on typographic behaviour on screen, such as time-based fonts, type as icon, space and navigation issues and the fluidity of type. The studio also explores whether fonts can adapt themselves to the environment in which they are viewed, for example on the monitor, television, WAP or in 3-D space.

The advent of Flash and Shockwave has allowed a much more in-depth investigation into type. In the near future amorphic and spatial graphic environments will be seen in which the animated graphic scale will be more practical with vector elements. The use of layers to create space, as introduced in Photoshop, will also be used more creatively in Flash.

1–2 Examples of the studio's investigation into visualizing space.

3–4 Snapshots from the studio's website.

5 Conversations in an internet chatroom are mapped out.

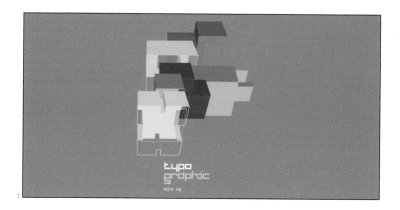

1

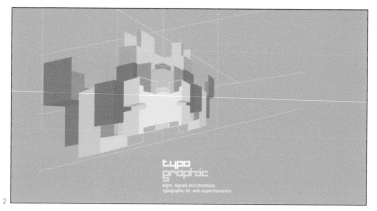

2

3
4

6

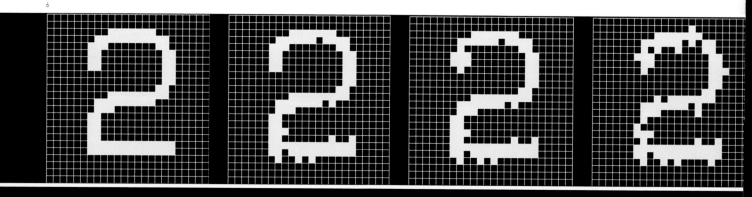

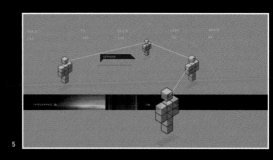

5

typographic 56

T 56

WHAT

SIGNS, SIGNALS AND DIRECTIONS WAS THE THEME SET
FOR THE 56TH STD **TYPOGRAPHIC MAGAZINE** . THIS WEBSITE
PRESENTS THE ARTICLES THAT WERE SUBMITTED UNDER
THAT THEME AND THE SUBSEQUENT EXPERIMENTS AND
IDEAS THAT HAVE EMERGED FROM OUR DISCUSSIONS.

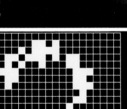

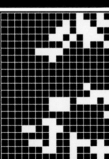

TYPOGRAPHIC 56

T 56

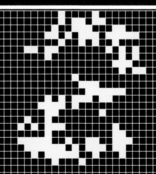

LINKS COMMENTS US OUR THOUGHTS DOWNLOADS

PUT A PIXEL IN THE BOX

SCORE TYPEFACE

0

^ YOUR EIGHT MOST RECENT CHOICES ^

6
Typographic 56

TypeDNA was developed
by Pete Everett during his
final year at the University
of Plymouth, UK. It is a
control panel that processes
all the keystrokes on the

user's keyboard and
turns them into unique
typographic profiles.
The information is stored
in a text file on the
user's machine.

Typography's form
changes according to its
environment and the
involvement of the viewer.
In 'typeDNA #2: typeMutate',
an existing letterform is

transformed according to a
simple set of rules. First, the
user selects a position on
the grid: if there is already
a pixel in that location, it
is deleted; if the cell is

empty but next to an
existing pixel, a new pixel
is created.

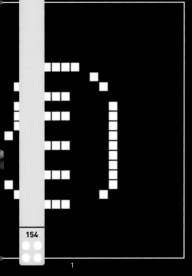

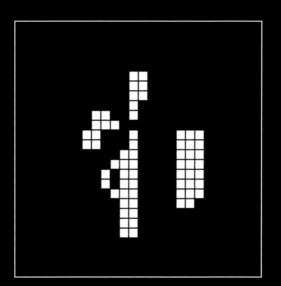

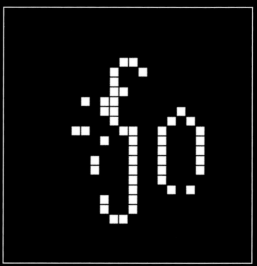

1

2

typeDNA #3 -> typeLife

to process a typeface using a personalised formula, we
need a method of mutation that is deterministic in nature.
such a process can be found in john conway's 'game of life'
whose rules are these:

Death -> If an occupied pixel has 0, 1, 4, 5, 6, 7, or 8
occupied neighbours, the pixel dies. (0, 1 neighbours: of
loneliness; 4 thru 8: of overcrowding).
Survival -> If an occupied pixel has two or three
neighbours, the pixel survives to the next generation.
Birth -> If an unoccupied pixel has three occupied
neighbours, it becomes occupied.

press any letter on the keyboard to use as a starting point,
then click the arrows to step through each 'generation' of
the letterform.

<u>back</u>

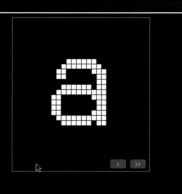

typeDNA #4 -> myType

'myType' combines the game of life and a user's
typographic profile to create personalised letterforms.

a reasonably complicated process, it takes each letterform
and processes it through up to 5 generations of the 'game
of life', using values squeezed out of your personal profile
as the rules for birth, survival and death (values which have
been converted into a 32-bit binary strings, then repeatedly
chopped up for easier consumption like a genetic
algorithm).

if you've been running the typeDNA screensaver, you'll be
able to enter your own e-mail address to retrieve and
process your own typographic profile. if you haven't, use
mine -> pete@deepend.co.uk

choose a font and a size, enter an e-mail address, then hit
'go!' -> once the letterforms have been processed, you can
zoom in on them for closer inspection.

<u>back</u>

choose a font: [Chicago   ]
choose a font size: ◁ 24 ▷
enter e-mail address:
pete@deepend.co.uk

3

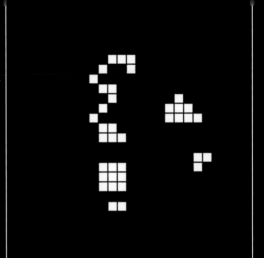

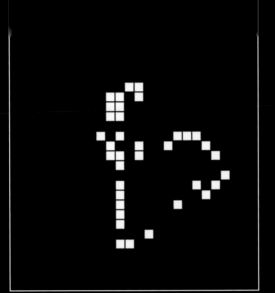

1–2 TypeDNA #3:typeLife suggests that to process a typeface using a personalized formula, a method of mutation that is deterministic in nature is needed. Such a method is found in John Conway's 'Game of Life', which has three rules. If a pixel has 0,1,4,5,6,7 or 8 occupied neighbours on the grid, the pixel dies (0–1 neighbours and it dies of loneliness, 4–8 neighbours and it dies from overcrowding). If a pixel has 2 or 3 neighbours, it survives to the next generation. If an unoccupied cell is selected that has 3 occupied neighbours, it becomes occupied. Signs and symbols navigate the user through the information, using spatial depth and time as the underlying considerations.

3–4 TypeDNA #4:myType combines the 'Game of Life' and a user's typographic profile to create personalized letterforms.

4

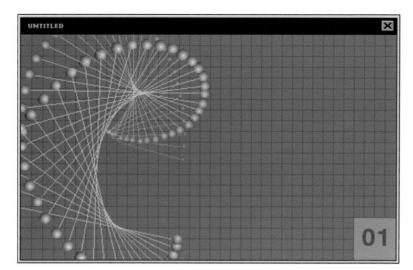

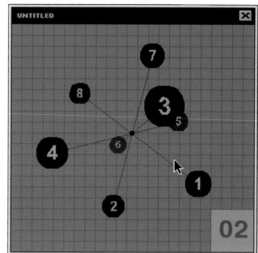

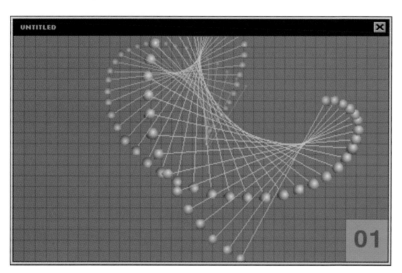

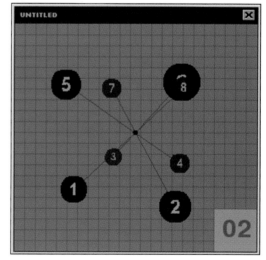

Wireframe Studio

'Conductors of multimedia', designers at Wireframe Studio consider themselves a work in progress. These six 'exercises' show great potential for visualizing information. Throughout the exercises, there is repeated emphasis on tools that allow users to easily manipulate all three dimensions. Finely tuned to the proximity of the user's mouse, Wireframe interfaces simulate a physical 'give', almost as if referring back to such older pressure-based technologies as spring-driven umbrella latches or bathroom scales.

All structural elements allow the user a 360-degree perspective, whether expressed through isometric layouts or the use of rotation. →

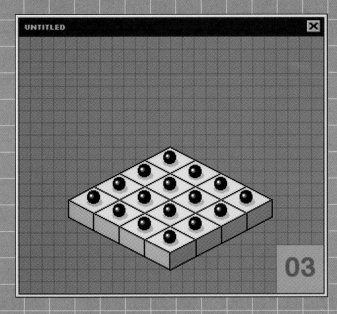

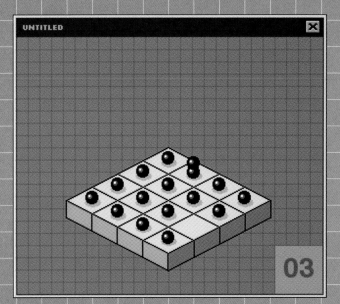

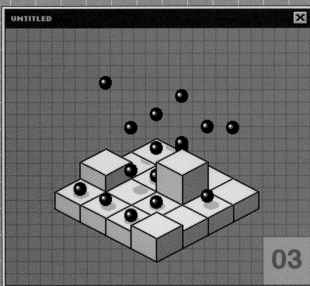

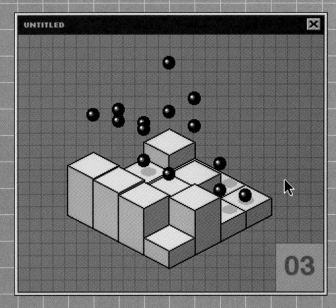

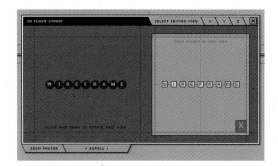

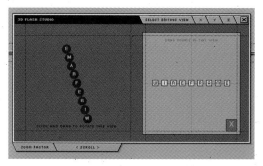

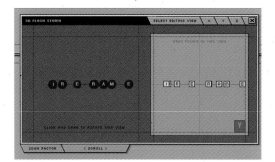

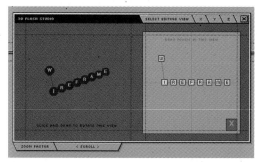

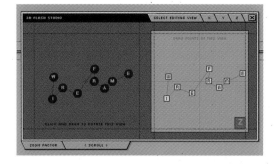

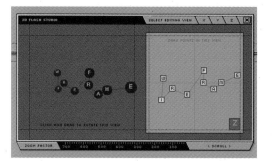

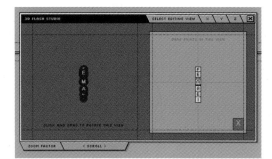

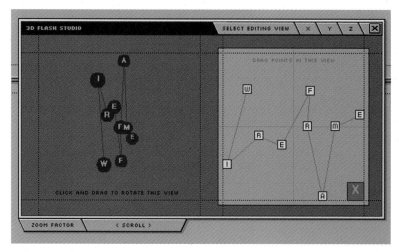

Wireframe Studio

In exercise three (p. 157), mouseover triggers squares to catapult balls that fall under gravity's pull. Users can manipulate connected balls into unique configurations and then view the resulting structure's complexity horizontally and vertically, but also from a third perspective that shows depth.

In Crowd Behaviour (opposite, bottom), the fixed x- and y-axes are skewed toward the user while a crowd of figures mingle at right angles to the viewer. These units are 'semi-intelligent' and can, for example, detect a collision course. The properties of gravity are playfully applied to each interface to illustrate the user's sense of movement. When the units jump vertically, they land in a way that suggests the natural give of body mechanics under the weight of gravity.

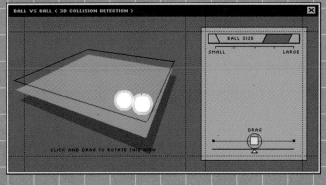

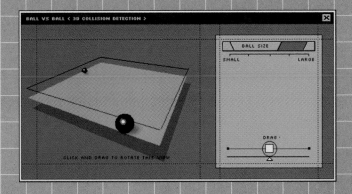

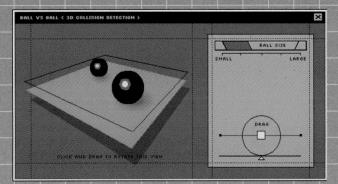

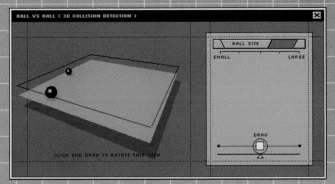

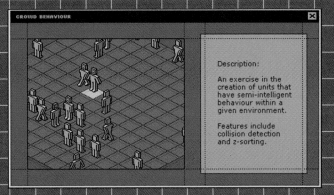

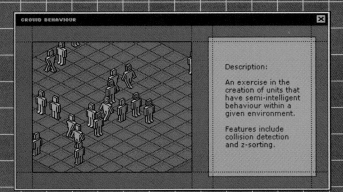

BALL VS BALL < 3D COLLISION DETECTION >

BALL SIZE
SMALL   LARGE

CLICK AND DRAG TO ROTATE THIS VIEW

DRAG

CROWD BEHAVIOUR

Description:

An exercise in the creation of units that have semi-intelligent behaviour within a given environment.

Features include collision detection and z-sorting.

Equator Interdisciplinary Research Collaboration
Combining the Physical and Digital Worlds

Focusing on the integration of the physical and the digital and supporting the variety of possible relationships between the two worlds are the aims of the Equator Interdisciplinary Research Collaboration between eight UK institutions. The unit's 'experience projects' test new technologies, practise new design and evaluation methods, engage users in the research process and publicly demonstrate the results. They are application-based activities, concentrating on supporting users and exploiting the methods, models and technologies of Equator research challenges. One such effort, known as 'City', treats the city and information in a way that deliberately blurs the boundaries between physical and digital media.

Concept What makes a city meaningful to researchers at Equator is not just the bricks and mortar of a constructed space, but our understanding and use of it. For example, the physical space of a street, building or room is just one of the areas that affords activity in, and interpretation of, a city. In City, researchers from Glasgow, Bristol, University College London, Nottingham and Southampton are weaving digital media into the physical streets, buildings and artefacts of a city. The initial development of this project uses Glasgow and the context of an exhibition on designer and architect Charles Rennie Mackintosh, but will soon extend to cover other people, information and places in the city.

Structure The images presented on these pages portray the users as avatars – representations of humans in a digital environment – and show the view they would have of one another.

Context The developers combine mobile computers, hypermedia and virtual-reality (VR) applications into one larger system to explore the ways people can interact and maintain awareness of each other even when spatially separated and using a variety of interactive devices (portable computing and communication products and other newly researched wearable and embedded technologies) and media (text, sound and static and moving images).

Navigation Current explorations involve one person using a wearable computer, a second person using text and graphics and a third person using VR. Each person can have hypermedia documents delivered to them for browsing, and they can all speak to each other and see the others' locations. The hypermedia and VR users each control a laptop, while the wearable user controls a handheld (PDA), and has his or her position in a room tracked by ultrasound.

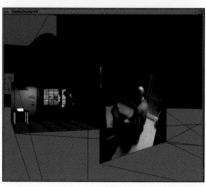

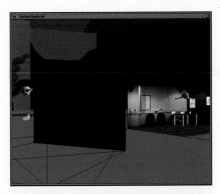

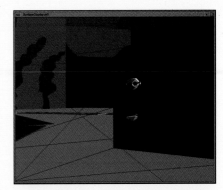

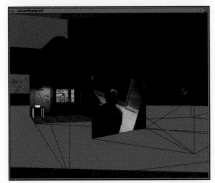

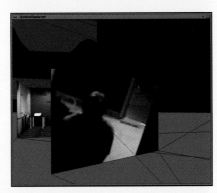

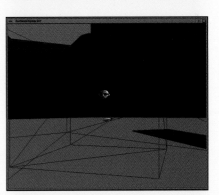

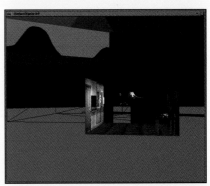

1–4
Ici la Lune

Although the screen cannot be treated as a sheet of paper, 'screen culture' is highly influenced by print culture. Ici la Lune experiments with typography's function of presenting content with particular attention to interface and ergonomics.

Ici's models are represented through three media: the internet, CD-ROM and television, using primarily Flash and Shockwave. Each navigation system creates a virtual space for type to exist in three dimensions, thus visually interpreting and shaping the contents and how they are communicated. Data displayed through these systems encourages the involvement of the user in navigating within the structure while accessing information.

Aiming to produce their own interface vocabulary, Ici la Lune created navigation systems specific to different applications. **1–2** In 'Scroll Intégral', the user can scroll the contents in any direction by simply moving the mouse on the screen. Navigation takes place in an area whose limits are outside the screen. **3–4** An image animation that scrolls vertically or horizontally, 'Scroll Dynamique' has a speed related to the movement of the image.

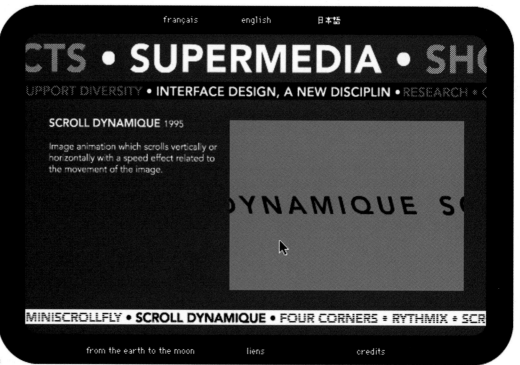

1

3

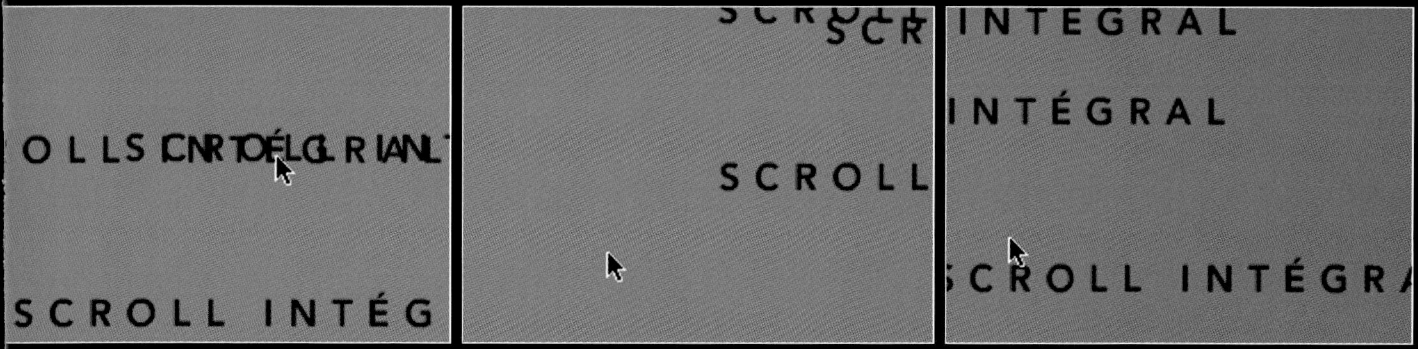

O L L S C R T O É L G R I A N L

SCROLL INTÉG

S C R O L L

S C R

INTEGRAL

INTÉGRAL

SCROLL INTÉGRA

2

MIQUE SCRO

YNAMIQUE S

SCROLL DYN

4

TEXTE ÉLASTIQUE 1995

The "elastic text" presents the text in a dynamic way: the size of the characters depends on the position of the mouse on the text itself.

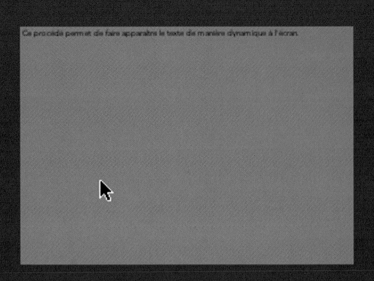

1

GYROSCOPI 1997

3D animation concept based upon the idea of the mobile, giving easy access to different contents.

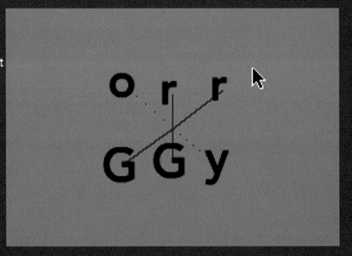

2

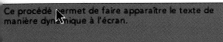

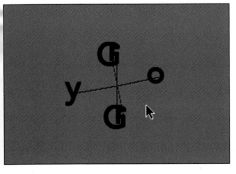
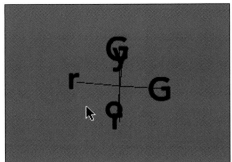
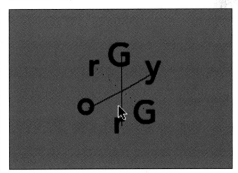

1–2
Ici la Lune

1 'Texte Élastique' changes
the size of the letters
depending on the position
of the mouse.

2 'Gyroscopi' is a 3-D
animation giving easy
access to different contents,
based on the idea of the
mobile phone.

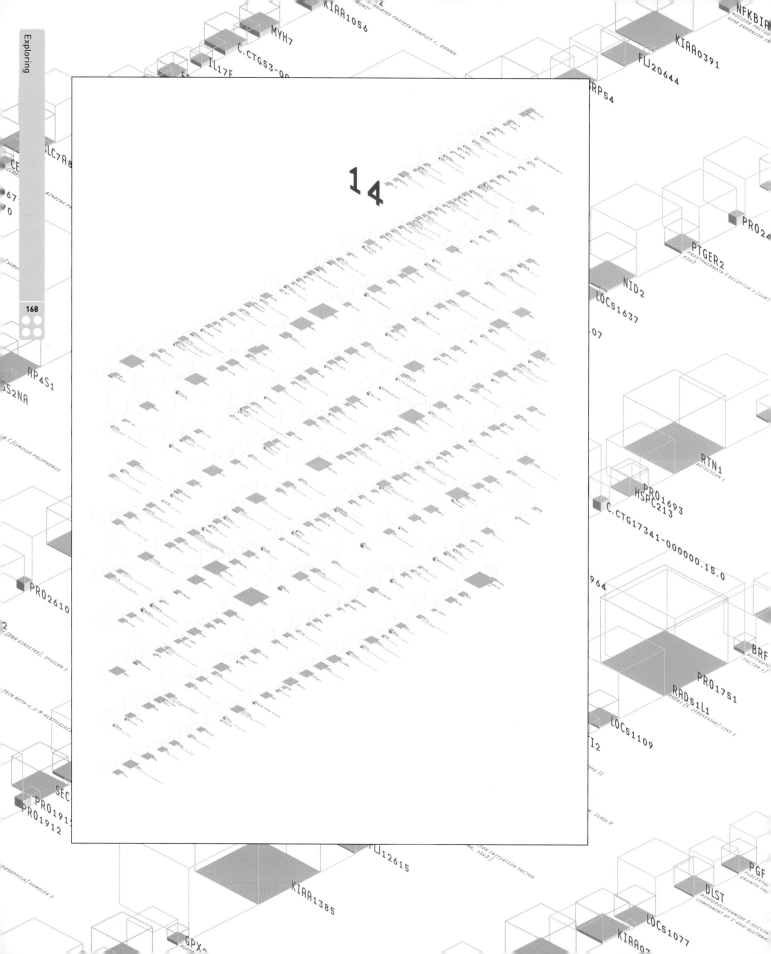

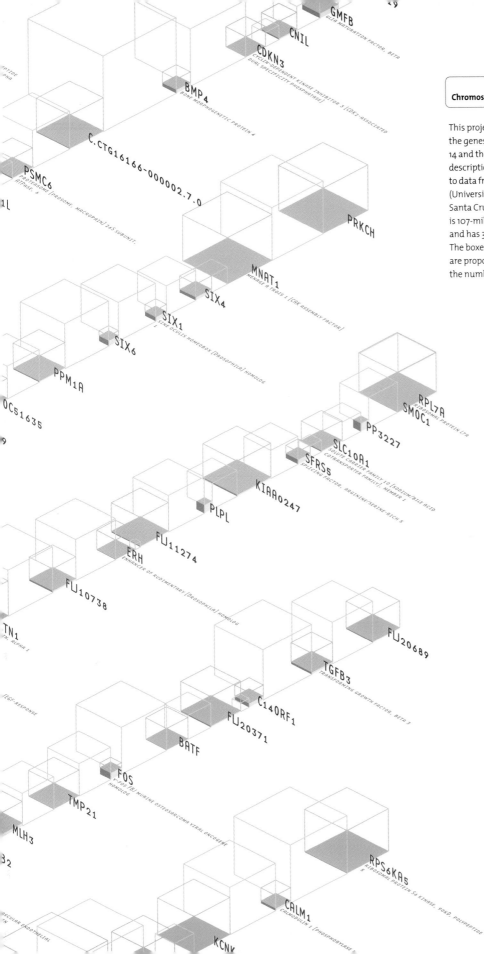

Chromosome 14

This project visualizes the genes on chromosome 14 and their relevant descriptions. According to data from UCSC (University of California at Santa Cruz), Chromosome 14 is 107-million-letters long and has 347 identified genes. The boxes in the illustrations are proportional in size to the number of letters for that gene code. Yellow wireframe boxes signify a gap between genes, an area where the letters are considered 'junk DNA.' The blue areas show where genes exist. The blue wireframe boxes are proportional in size to the start and end point of the gene within the sequence of letters.

.CCTG.T.A...TGCAG..GCACGTATTG.A
TCCCA.CC...ATGGTC...T.CGTACAT.A
CCC.GCTTACG..GC..TGG.ACGT.C..CA
C.CT..T.AC.GTG.AGTGGC.C.TATTGC.
CC.T.CTTACGGTGC.GTGGCA....TT.C.
C.CT..T.AC.GTG.AGTAGG.C.TATTGC

CCCCGCTTACGGTGCAGTGGCACGTATATCA

ACGGTG

CGTCTAG

GTGCGGC

CCCTGCTTACGGTGCAGTGGCACGTATTTCA

GCGTAAC

GCAACA

TGATTAG

GTGTAAT

CCCTGCTTACGGTGCAGTGGCACGTATAGCA

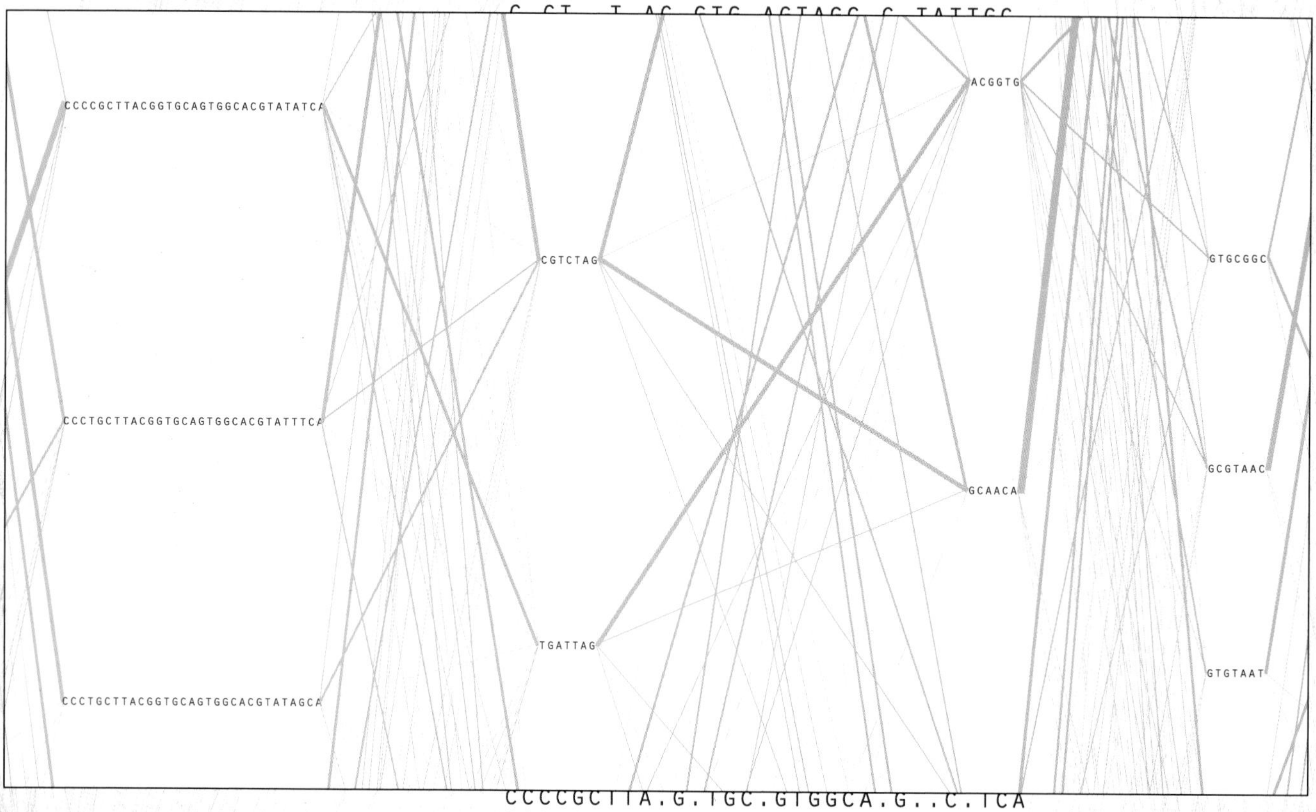

CCCCGCTTA.G.TGC.GTGGCA.G..C.TCA
CCC.GC..ACGG.GCAGTGGCACGTA..TC.

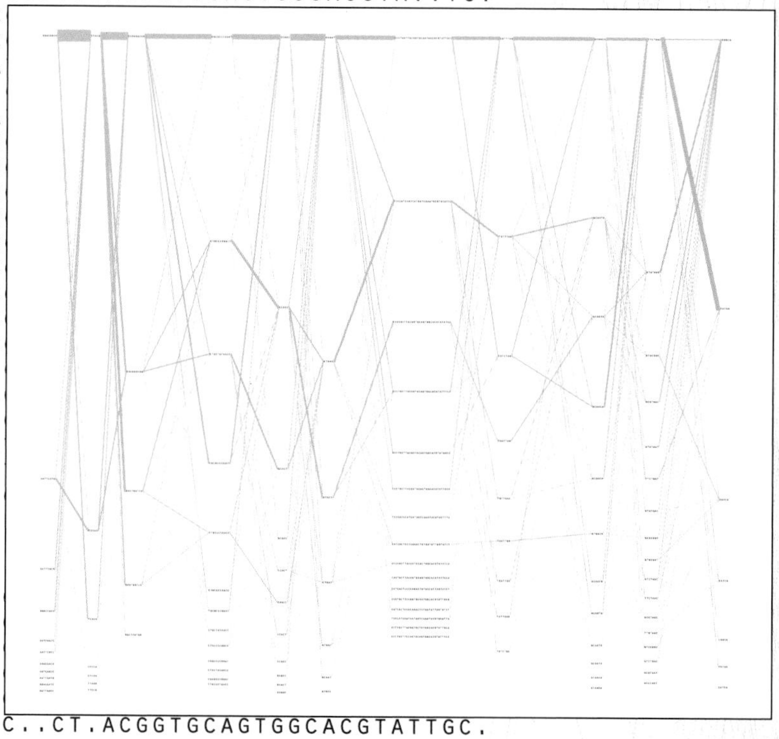

..C..CT.ACGGTGCAGTGGCACGTATTGC.
C....CTTACGGTGC.GTGGCACGT.TTGCA
C.C.GCTTACG..G.AGTGGCACGTAT.GCA
.CCCATC.A.CATGGT.T.ATGCGTACAT.A
C.CTGCT...CG.TGC.GTGGCACGTAT.GCA
CCCTGCTT..G.TGC.GTGGCA.G.ATTGCA
CCCTGCTTACG.TGC.GTGGCA.G..T.GCA
T.CCAT.CATCATG.T.GAATGCGTA..TTA
CCC.G.T.ACGGTGCA.T.GCACGTATTGC.

. .
AC
. .
. A
. .
. CA
A
..GA.
.T..C
A..C.
AC...
..A.T
C..A.
C...C
C.G..
..G.C
..ACT
..GAT
C.G.T
.CGA.
.C.AT
A..CT
C..AC
A.AC.
.TAC.
A.G.T
.TGA.
C..AT
..GAC
.T.AC
A.A.T
C.G.C
C.GA.
.T.CT
CTG.C
CTGC.
AC.AT
.TGAT
C.GAC
A.ACC
A.ACT
CT.AC
ATGA.
CCGA.
.TGAC
.CGAT
CTGA.
ATAC.
CC.AT
ATA.T
C.GAT
AT.CT
.TACT
CCGAT
CTGAT
CTGAC

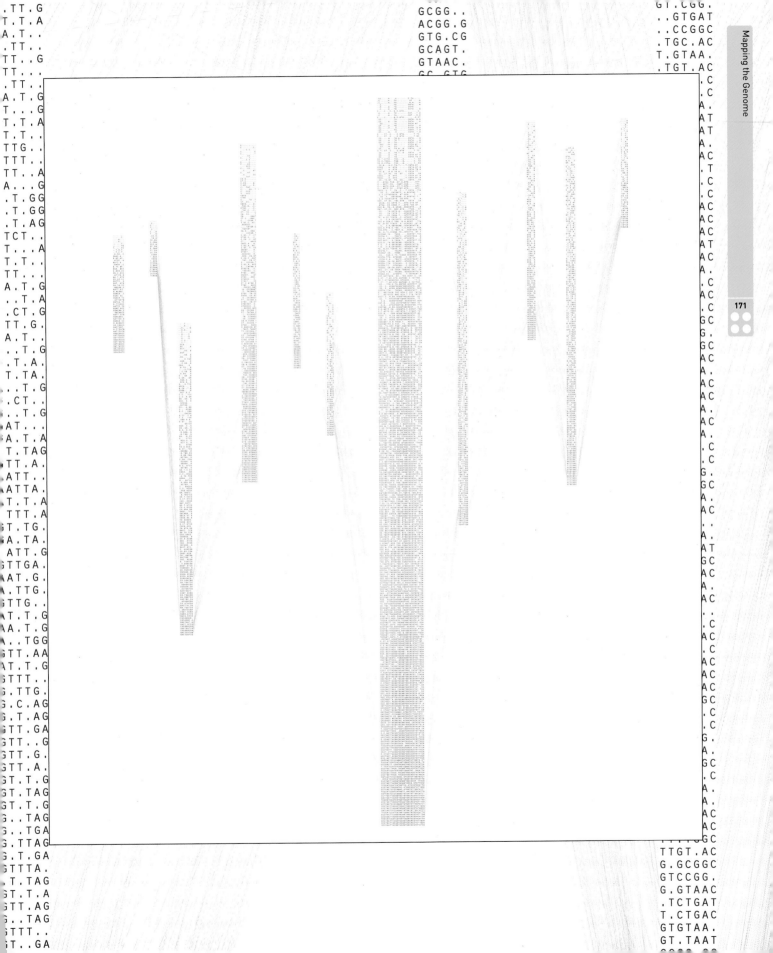

Glossary

Backbone network The top level in a hierarchical network, a backbone network maximizes user connectivity and accommodates a variety of end-system technologies.

Bulletin-board system An electronic message database.

Cathode Ray Tube (CRT) An electrical device for displaying images by illuminating phosphor dots with a scanned electron beam behind a glass screen. CRTs are found in computer monitors and televisions.

Client A computer system or program that requests and receives information from another computer system or program (a server) by way of a protocol.

Common Gateway Interface (CGI) The standard interface that World Wide Web clients and servers use to communicate data for the creation of interactive applications.

Edge The relationship between two or more data elements (nodes).

Ethernet A geographically limited network.

Extensible Markup Language (XML) A simple and universal language for use on the web.

Flash Application and file format produced by Macromedia, providing tools for developing interactive vector-based graphics and animation for the World Wide Web. The file format is used for delivering animation movies on the web.

Graph A diagram that illustrates a relationship between two or more sets of data, usually quantitative.

Hypermedia Similar to hypertext, but also contains image, sound and video elements.

Hypertext A term coined by Ted Nelson in 1965 for a collection of documents containing cross-references (or 'links') that, with the aid of a browser program, allow the reader to move easily from one document to another. It permits multiple authors, reading paths and collaborative communication.

HyperText Markup Language (HTML) The standard language used for creating hypermedia documents within the World Wide Web.

HyperText Transfer Protocol (HTTP) The standard protocol that World Wide Web clients and servers use to communicate.

Internet The global computer network. It is a three-level hierarchy composed of backbone networks, mid-level networks and stub networks. These include commercial ('.com' or '.co'), university ('.ac' or '.edu'), research ('.org', '.net') and military ('.mil') networks.

Link A reference from a point in one hypertext document to a place in the same document or to a point in another document. A browser generally displays a hyperlink visually, using a different colour, font or style (such as underline). When the user activates the link, usually by clicking on it with the mouse, the browser shows the target of the link.

Liquid Crystal Display (LCD) A display created by placing liquid crystal between a pair of transparent electrodes. Voltage is applied between the electrodes, which activates the liquid crystal and changes the phase of the light passing through it to display pixels, digits, characters or images on watches, mobile telephones, calculators and portable computers.

Mid-level or regional network A network that makes up the second level of the internet hierarchy, connecting the stub network to the backbone network.

Mouseover An action whereby the computer user moves the mouse pointer icon over an element on the computer screen, causing a change in the element's colour, shade or shape and signifying that a further action, most likely the click of a mouse button, is needed to activate that element.

Multipurpose Internet Mail Extension (MIME) A standard extension for multipart, multimedia electronic mail messages and World Wide Web hypertext documents on the internet. MIME allows the transfer of non-textual data, such as graphics and audio elements.

Network News Transfer Protocol (NNTP) A protocol for the distribution, retrieval and posting of Usenet news articles over the internet.

Node A connection point in a network, either a redistribution point or an end point for data transmissions. In general, a node is programmed or engineered to recognize, process or forward transmissions to other nodes. Also, a data point or vertex in a graph.

Open Systems Interconnection (OSI) A standard description or 'reference model' of how messages should be transmitted between any two points in a telecommunication network.

Packet A unit of data sent across a network.

Personal Digital Assistant (PDA) A small hand-held computer used to write notes, track appointments and store contact information. A notepad, address book and diary in one digital format.

Photoshop Software developed by Adobe Systems, Inc that manipulates and edits images.

Pixel Short for picture element, this is the smallest visible rectangular area of an image on a computer monitor.

Practical Extraction and Report Language (Perl) Developed by Larry Wall in 1987, Perl is a general-purpose programming language often used for scanning text and printing formatted reports.

Protocol A set of rules explaining how to transmit data, especially across a network.

Scalability How well a solution to a problem will work when the size or complexity of the problem increases. For example, a central computer server with ten clients may perform adequately, however, with a thousand clients it might fail to meet response-time requirements. Or, a graphing system may display one hundred nodes legibly, but might not be able to show over a thousand nodes clearly.

Server A program that performs the tasks requested by the client. The connection between client and server is normally by means of message passing, often over a network, and uses some protocol to encode the client's requests and the server's responses.

Shockwave A program developed by Macromedia for viewing files created with the application Macromedia Director. Shockwave is freely available as a plug-in for the Netscape Navigator web browser.

Standard Generalized Markup Language (SGML) A generic markup language for representing documents, SGML describes the relationship between a document's content and its structure.

Stub network The bottom level in a hierarchical network, which only carries packets to and from local hosts.

Transmission Control Protocol (TCP) The most common protocol that provides a reliable connection to the ethernet and internet.

Uniform Resource Locater (URL) A standardized way of identifying different documents, media and network services on the World Wide Web.

Usenet A bulletin-board system supported mainly by Unix computer systems and users who post and read articles on the database. Begun in 1979 by Steve Bellovin, Jim Ellis, Tom Truscott and Steve Daniel, it has grown to become international in scope and was probably the largest decentralized information utility in existence before the introduction of the World Wide Web.

Virtual Reality Markup Language (VRML) A language for describing three-dimensional hypermedia objects in virtual-reality environments.

Wireless Application Protocol (WAP) A standard protocol for procedures that use wireless communication, such as accessing the internet from a mobile telephone.

World Wide Web A distributed information retrieval system for linked hypertext files that originated in the CERN High-Energy Physics laboratories in Geneva, Switzerland in 1991.

Bibliography

Bounford, Trevor and Alastair Campbell. *Digital Diagrams: How to Design and Present Statistical Information Effectively* (New York: Watson-Guptill Publications, 2000).

Card, Stuart K., Jock D. Mackinlay and Ben Schneiderman. *Readings in Information Visualization: Using Vision to Think* (San Francisco, CA: Morgan Kaufmann Publishers, 1999).

Dodge, Martin and Rob Kitchin. *Atlas of Cyberspace* (Reading, MA: Addison Wesley Higher Education Group, 2001).

Dodge, Martin and Rob Kitchin. *Mapping Cyberspace* (New York: Routledge, 2000).

Harris, Robert L. *Information Graphics: A Comprehensive Illustrated Reference* (New York: Oxford University Press Inc., 2000).

Jacobson, Robert E., ed. *Information Design* (Cambridge, MA: The MIT Press, 1999).

Spence, Robert. *Information Visualization* (Reading, MA: Addison Wesley Higher Education Group, 2000).

Tufte, Edward R. *The Visual Display of Quantitative Information* (Cheshire, CT: Graphics Press, 2nd ed., 2001).

Tufte, Edward R. *Visual Explanations: Images and Quantities, Evidence and Narrative* (Cheshire, CT: Graphics Press, 1997).

Tufte, Edward R. *Envisioning Information* (Cheshire, CT: Graphics Press, 1990).

Ware, Colin. *Information Visualization: Perception for Design* (San Francisco, CA: Morgan Kaufmann Publishers, 2000).

Wildbur, Peter and Michael Burke. *Information Graphics: Innovative Solutions in Contemporary Design* (London: Thames & Hudson, Ltd., 1999).

Wilkinson, Leland. *Statistics and Computing: The Grammar of Graphics* (New York: Springer-Verlag, 1999).

Wurman, Richard Saul. *Information Anxiety 2* (Indianapolis, IN: New Riders, 2nd ed., 2001).

Wurman, Richard Saul. *Understanding USA* (TED Conferences Inc., 1999).

Wurman, Richard Saul. Peter Bradford, ed. *Information Architects* (New York: Graphis Press: 1996).

Wurman, Richard Saul. *Information Anxiety: What to Do When Information Doesn't Tell You What You Need to Know* (New York: Bantam Dell Publishing Group, 1990).

Credits and Websites

The Brain
http://www.thebrain.com

Chromosome 14
Ben Fry, Aesthetics and Computation Group, MIT Media Lab, US
http://acg.media.mit.edu/people/fry/chromosomes/

City'O'Scope
Macrofocus, Switzerland
http://www.macrofocus.com

Cooperative Association for Internet Data Analysis (CAIDA)
Supercomputer Center, University of California, US
• http://www.caida.org
• http://www.caida.org/tools/visualization/walrus/

Datascapes
Lise Anne Couture and Hani Rashid, Asymptote, US
http://www.asymptote-architecture.com

eBizinsights
Stephen Eick, Visual Insights, US
http://www.visualinsights.com

Equator Interdisciplinary Research Collaboration
http://www.dcs.gla.ac.uk/equator/city.html

ET Map
Hsinchun Chen, Artificial Intelligence Laboratory,

University of Arizona, US
http://ai.bpa.arizona.edu

e-Types
Denmark
http://www.e-types.com

GameLab
Eric Zimmerman and Peter Lee, US
http://www.gmlb.com

GraphViz
AT & T Labs – Research
http://www.research.att.com/sw/tools/graphviz/overview.html

Human Extensibility
Paul Adams, Department of Geography, Texas A & M University, US
http://geog.tamu.edu/faculty/adams/Frame.htm

Hyperbolic Space
Tamara Munzner, Compaq
Systems Research Center,
Stamford University, US
• http://www-graphics.
stanford.edu/~munzner/
• http://graphics.stanford.edu/
papers/h3/
• http://graphics.stanford.edu/
papers/h3cga/

Ici La Lune
France
http://www.icilalune.com

Internet Connectivity Graph
Hal Burch and Bill Cheswick, US
http://www.cs.bell-labs.com/
who/ches/map/index.html

The Internet Weather Report
• http://www.mids.org/
weather/
• http://www.quarterman.
com/~jsq/index.html

Lighthouse
Anton Leuski and James
Allan, Center for Intelligent
Information Retrieval,
University of Massachusetts
at Amherst, US
http://toowoomba.cs.umass.
edu/%7Eleouski/lighthouse/

Loom2
Judith Donath and Hyun-Yeul
Lee, Sociable Media Group,
MIT Media Lab, US
http://smg.www.media.mit.
edu/projects/loom2

Map of the Market
Martin Wattenberg,
SmartMoney.com, US
http://www.smartmoney.com/
marketmap

Map.net
Visual Net, Antarcti.ca Systems,
Canada and US
• http://maps.map.net/start
• http://antarcti.ca/

Media Neutral
Thomas Müller, Razorfish, US
http://www.razorfish.com

MONO*crafts
Yugo Nakamura, Japan
• http://www.yugop.com
• http://www.shift.jp.org/
• http://www.b-architects.
com/

MTV2
Digit, UK
• http://www.mtv2.co.uk
• http://www.digitlondon.com
• http://www.stoprefresh.com

**NicheWorks + Exploratory
Data Visualizer (EDV)**
Graham Wills,
Bell Laboratories, US
http://www.bell-labs.com/
project/visualinsights

Organic Information Design
Ben Fry, Aesthetics and
Computation Group,
MIT Media Lab, US
http://acg.media.mit.edu/
people/fry/

**Organizational
Network Mapping**
Valdis Krebs, Krebs &
Associates, US
http://www.orgnet.com

PeopleGarden
Rebecca Xiong, Sociable Media
Group, MIT Media Lab, US
http://smg.media.mit.edu/pap
ers/Xiong/pgarden_uist99.pdf

**Populated Information
Terrains (PITS)**
Steve Benford and
Dave Snowdon, University
of Nottingham, UK
http://www.crg.cs.nott.ac.uk/
research/applications/pits/

Rhizome
US
http://www.rhizome.org

Self-Organizing Maps
Teuvo Kohonen, Neural
Networks Research Centre,
Helsinki University of
Technology, Finland
http://websom.hut.fi/
websom/

Semantic Constellation
Chaomei Chen, Department
of Information Systems
and Computing,
Brunel University, UK
http://www.brunel.ac.uk/
~cssrccc2

Sinnzeug
Stephan Huber, Ralph Ammer
and Birte Steffan, Germany
http://www.cybrig.org

SmartDraw
http://www.smartdraw.com

SQWID
Scott McCrickard, Colleen
Kehoe and Amy Opalak,
Georgia Institute of
Technology, US
http://www.cc.gatech.edu/
grads/m/Scott.McCrickard/
sqwid/

Starlight
John Risch, Pacific Northwest
National Laboratory, US
http://www.pnl.gov/nsd/
commercial/starlight/

TableLens
Inxight Software, US
• http://www.inxight.com
• http://www.tablelens.com

Thinkmap
Thinkmap Inc and Plumb
Design, US
http://www.thinkmap.com

Traceroute Software
Stephen Coast, US
http://www.fractalus.com/
steve/stuff/ipmap/

Trailmaps
Matthew Chalmers,
Department of Computing
Science, University
of Glasgow, UK
http://www.dcs.gla.ac.uk/~
matthew/

Turux
Dextro, Austria
http://www.turux.org

Typographic 56
UK
http://www.typographic56.
co.uk

URLGRAPH
Kevin Palfreyman, UK
http://www.comp.lancs.ac.uk/
computing/users/kev/
computing/project/graph/
graph.html

Visual Explanations
XPLANE, US
http://www.xplane.com

Visualizing Spreadsheets
Ed Chi and Stuart Card, Xerox
Palo Alto Research Center, US
http://www.cs.umn.edu/~echi/

Web Stalker
Matthew Fuller and Escape, UK
• http://www.backspace.org/
iod/escape.html
• http://www.archimuse.com/
mw98/beyondinterface/fuller
_fr.html

Web Traffic Project
Antoine Visonneau,
Center for Design Informatics,
Harvard University Graduate
School of Design, US
http://research3.gsd.harvard.
edu/webtraffic/prototypes.
htm

Website User Paths (VISVIP)
John Cugini, Visualization and
Virtual Reality Group, National
Institute of Standards and
Technology, US
http://www.itl.nist.gov/iaui/
vvrg/cugini/webmet/visvip/
vv-home.html

Webtracer
NullPointer, UK
• http://www.nullpointer.
co.uk/
• http://www.dividebyzero.org
• http://rhizome.org/object.
rhiz?2330

Wireframe Studio
http://www.wireframe.co.za

Index

Adams, Paul 109
Aesthetics and Computation Group, US 30
Allan, James 77
Ammer, Ralph 141
Anemone 30, 36–37
Antarti.ca 81
Artificial Intelligence Laboratory, US 78
Asymptote 61, 70–73

Bell Laboratories, US 83, 96
Benford, Steve 127
The Brain 120–21
Brunel University 110
Burch, Hal 83
Business 2.0 122–23

Card, Stuart 67
Carnegie Mellow University, US 83
Cartesian grid 60
Center for Design Informatics, US 65
Center for Intelligent Information Retrieval, US 77
Chalmers, Matthew 23
Chen, Chaomei 110
Chen, Hsinchun 78
Cheswick, Bill 83
Chi, Ed 67
The Chicago Tribune 100–01
Chromosome 14 168–71
Chromosome 22 119
'City' 160–63
City'O'Scope 90–91
Coast, Stephen 43
Cognitive Science Laboratory, US 86
Columbus, Christopher 19
Computer Graphics Laboratory, US 26
Conway, John 155
Cooperative Association for Internet Data Analysis (CAIDA) 24, 28–29
Couture, Lise Anne 70
Cugini, John 20

Datascapes 70–73
Dextro 142
Digit 50

eBizinsights 94–95
Eick, Stephen 95
Equator Interdisciplinary Research Collaboration 160–63
Escape 55
ET Map 78–79
e-Types 150–51
Everett, Peter 153
Every Image Software 144–45
Excite 77
Exploratory Data Visualizer (EDV) 96–101

Flash 124–25
Fry, Ben 30–37, 119, 168–71
Fuller, Matthew 55

Gall 9
GameLab 128–29
Georgia Institute of Technology, US 74
GIF 124–25
Goode 9
Google 47, 77, 105
GraphViz 132–35
Green, Colin 55
Gutenberg, Johann 6
'Gyroscopi' 166–67

Harvard Graduate School of Design, US 65
HTML 55, 130
Huber, Stephan 141
Human Extensibility 108–09
Hyperbolic Space 26–27

Ici La Lune 164–67
Internet Industry Partnerships 116
Internet Mapping Project 82–83
Internet Weather Report 19, 56–57
Inxight Software, US 39

Java 35, 57, 74, 86, 91

Kehoe, Colleen 74
Kohonen, Teuvo 45
Krebs, Valdis 116–19

Lee, Peter 129
Leuski, Anton 77
Lighthouse 76–77
Loom2 112–15

McCrickard, Scott 74
Mackintosh, Charles Rennie 160
Macrofocus 91
Map of the Market 92–93
Map.net 80–81
Maya Software 71
Media Neutral 88–89
Mercator 9
Microsoft 48
MIT Media Lab, US 30, 106, 112
MONO*crafts 148–49
MTV2 50–53
Müller, Thomas 89
Munzner, Tamara 26, 27

Nakamura, Yugo 148–49
National Center for Supercomputing Applications, US 62
National Institute of Standards and Technology, US 20
NatWest.com 89
New York Stock Exchange 61
NicheWorks 96–101
NullPointer 47

Opalak, Amy 74
Organic Information Design 30–37
Organizational Network Mapping 118–19

Pablo Research Group, US 62
Pacific Northwest National Laboratory, US 84
Palfreyman, Kevin 40
PeopleGarden 106
Plumb Design Visual Thesaurus 86
Pope, Simon 55
Populated Information Terrain (PIT) 105, 126–27
Princeton University, US 86

Rashid, Hani 70
Razorfish 89
Reed, Daniel 62
Rhizome 48, 144–47
Risch, John 84

San Diego Supercomputer Center, US 29
Saussure, Ferdinand de 7
'Scroll Dynamique' 164–65
'Scroll Intégral' 164–65
Search Query Weighted Information Display (SQWID) 74–75
Self-Organizing Maps 44–45
Semantic Constellations 110–11
Sinnzeug 140–41
SmartDraw 130–31
SmartMoney.com 92
Snowdon, Dave 127
Sociable Media Group, US 112
Spiral 146
Stanford University, US 26
Starlight 84–85
StarryNight 146–47
Steffan, Birte 141

TableLens 38–39
Tendril 30, 34–35
'Texte Elastique' 166–67
Thinkmap 86–87
Traceroute Software 42–43, 83
Trailmaps 22–23
Turux 142–43
Twain, Mark 30
TypeDNA 152–53
Typographic 56 152–55

University College London 43
University of Arizona, US 78
University of California, US 29
University of Glasgow, UK 23
University of Illinois, US 62
University of Massachusetts, US 77
University of Nottingham, UK 127
University of Plymouth, UK 153
University of Technology, Helsinki, Finland 45
URLGRAPH 40–41
Usenet 105, 112

Valence 30–33
Vellum 109
Visonneau, Antoine 65
Visual Explanations 122–25
Visual Insight 95
Visual Net 81
Visualization and Virtual Reality Group, US 20
Visualizing Spreadsheets 66–69
VRML 65, 71, 110

Walrus 24–25
Wattenberg, Martin 92
Web Stalker 54–55
Web Traffic Project 64–65
Web Traffic Skyscrapers 62–63
WebFan 107
Webmetrics 20
Website User Paths 20–21
WEBSOM 45
Webtracer 46–49
Wills, Graham 96
Wired 124
Wireframe Studio 156–59
World Wide Web 12, 18, 19, 40, 62, 74
WorldNet database 86
Wurman, Richard Saul 70

Xerox Palo Alto Research Center, US 39, 67
Xiong, Rebecca 106–07
XML 124
XPLANE 122–25

Yahoo! 77, 78, 105